AnimalWays

Beetles

AnimalWays

Beetles

Marc Zabludoff

Marshall Cavendish
Benchmark
New York

With thanks to Dr. Dan Wharton, director of the Central Park Wildlife Center, for his expert review of this manuscript.

Marshall Cavendish Benchmark
99 White Plains Road
Tarrytown, NY 10591
www.marshallcavendish.us

Library of Congress Cataloging-in-Publication Data

Zabludoff, Marc.
Beetles / by Marc Zabludoff.
p. cm. — (Animalways)
Summary: "An exploration of the life cycle, diet, behavior, anatomy, and conservation status of beetles"—Provided by publisher.
Includes bibliographical references and index.
ISBN 978-0-7614-2532-8
1. Beetles—Juvenile literature. I. Title. II. Series.
QL576.2.Z33 2007
595.76—dc22
2006038518

Publisher: Michelle Bisson
Art Director: Anahid Hamparian

Photo research by Candlepants Incorporated

Cover photo: BIOS/Borrell Bartomeu / Peter Arnold Inc.

The photographs in this book are used by permission and through the courtesy of:
Minden Pictures: Piotr Naskrecki, 2-3, 63; Michael & Patricia Fogden, 7 (bottom, third from right); Mark Moffett, 12, 24, 41, 50, 102, 54, 73, 74, 88, 91, 94, 99; Frans Lanting, 21, 96; Jef Meul/Foto Natura, 47; Mitsuhiko Imamori, 65; Tom Vezo, 69; Rob Reijnen/Foto Natura, 86. *Corbis*: Anthony Bannister/Gallo Images, 9; DK Limited, 22; Olivier Pojzman/ZUMA, 60. *Animals Animals*: David M. Dennis, 10; Patti Murray, 27; Brian P. Kenney, 71; E. R. Degginger, 77; Bill Beatty, 84. *Art Resource, NY*: Giraudon, 15. *Peter Arnold Inc.*: Helga Lade GmbH, Germany, 16; BIOS Gilson François, 19; F. Gilson, 28. *Photo Researchers Inc.*: Ted Kinsman, 35; A. Syred, 37; John Mitchell, 39; Eye of Science, 80. Super Stock: age fotostock, 82, back cover.

Printed in Malaysia
1 3 5 6 4 2

Contents

Animal Kingdom

CNIDARIANS

coral

ARTHROPODS
(animals with jointed limbs and external skeleton)

MOLLUSKS

squid

CRUSTACEANS

crab

ARACHNIDS

spider

INSECTS

BEETLES

MYRIAPODS

centipede

CARNIVORES

lion

SEA MAMMALS

whale

PRIMATES

orangutan

HERBIVORES
(5 orders)

elephant

PHYLA

ANNELIDS

earthworm

CHORDATES
(animals with
a dorsal
nerve chord)

ECHINODERMS

starfish

SUBPHYLA

VERTEBRATES
(animals with a
backbone)

CLASSES

FISH

fish

BIRDS

owls

MAMMALS

AMPHIBIANS

frog

REPTILES

snake

ORDERS

RODENTS

squirrel

INSECTIVORES

mole

MARSUPIALS

koala

SMALL MAMMALS
(several orders)

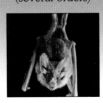

bat

1 A Beetle's Planet

It is a typical summer day, warm and quiet, in a typical American suburb. The soft buzzing of insects and the occasional raucous calls of crows are the only sounds. Nothing else is stirring in the afternoon heat.

But look closer. In front of a wood-and-brick two-story house, a shining rounded insect, nearly the size of a nickel, clings to the petals of a white rose. Its metallic green head gleams in the sunlight; so does its armored, coppery back.

Lower down on the plant, on a leaf, a ladybug has just landed. Its delicate black wings fold up and are immediately covered over by red armor. The ladybug starts its patrol, gorging itself on the small, slow white insects that drew it here.

Despite their different sizes, colors, and diet, both the ladybug and its larger neighbor are beetles, and they are not alone here. Many more beetles are nearby, though harder to see. Inside the spruce tree that stands on the lawn, a long, slender beetle chews out a tunnel for the eggs she is about to lay. As she gnaws at the wood, her long antennae lie flat against her white-spotted black shell.

APHID-EATING LADYBUGS ARE AMONG THE MOST FAMILIAR OF BEETLES, BUT THEY REPRESENT ONLY A TINY FRACTION OF THE BEETLES FOUND NEARLY EVERYWHERE ON EARTH.

On the ground, beneath a layer of spruce needles and blown leaves, a flat oval-shaped beetle hunts down a meal of newly hatched flies. Farther below, deep in the soil, hundreds of beetle larvae—immature forms of the insects—grow toward adulthood. They look more like toothed worms than like the adult beetles living above, but they have a grown-up hunger, and they are gnawing away at the tree's roots.

There are beetles in the house too, equally hidden. A few are growing ever so slowly inside the house's wooden beams. Others

BEETLE LARVAE OFTEN LIVE FOR MONTHS OR YEARS UNDERGROUND, FEEDING ON PLANT ROOTS.

are living secret lives in the darkness below the wooden floors, and still others have settled down beneath the carpet in the bedroom. Many more are in the kitchen, living in a dark paradise: a little-used bag of cornmeal that sits in the back of a cabinet.

Here, There, and Everywhere

Beetles have been crawling over the planet for a very long time. They have had nearly unimaginable centuries—hundreds of millions of years—to experiment with different body shapes and sizes, to try out different kinds of homes and foods, and to get used to different climates.

Today, in many ways, they are the true masters of our planet. There are more different types of beetles on Earth than of any other animal.

How many more? Imagine that we were somehow able to gather into a group a single representative from each of Earth's many different animals—one each of every kind of animal that crawls, walks, hops, slithers, or burrows over or under the ground; one each of every kind of animal that floats on or swims through the water.

One out of every four in that unruly mob would be a beetle. By themselves, the beetles would outnumber all the mammals, the reptiles, the birds, and the fish. In fact, they would outnumber all those other animals combined. They would outnumber all the spiders and all the other insects too.

There are more than 350,000 distinct beetle types, or species, inhabiting the Earth. Although they avoid the salty seas and the frozen middle of Antarctica, they thrive everywhere else, on every continent. They live under the ground, in and on the trees, deep in caves, and more than 16,000 feet (5,000 m) high in the Himalayas. They live in marshes, deserts, forests, and

THE WIDESPREAD AVAILABILITY OF PLANTS HAS ALLOWED LEAF-EATING BEETLES TO
SPREAD AROUND THE WORLD.

plains, in ponds, lakes, and streams, in cities and suburbs. They
have been found hibernating under more than 30 feet (10 m) of
snow and forging across the blistering sands of the Sahara.

Beetles will go wherever they can find something to eat,
and over the eons beetles have developed the ability to eat
nearly everything. They hunt down other insects and small animals, and they scavenge carrion, or dead animals, and animal
wastes. They eat all manner of plants and fungi, and devour all
the products that plants are turned into: flour, paper, furniture,
clothing—the list goes on and on and on. Beetles are among our
greatest rivals for food: they eat a big portion of the crops we
grow. At the same time, they are among the world's major

recyclers, and so they are indispensable to us. Without them, we would be awash in dead bodies, not to mention solid animal wastes, or dung, and other unpleasant substances.

Is it surprising that such remarkable animals are the stuff of legend?

Beetle Myths and Folktales

No people have ever thought more highly of an insect than did the ancient Egyptians, and the insect they held in greatest esteem was the dung beetle.

Dung beetles live off the solid wastes of animals, a diet that humans consider distasteful. But much of the animal kingdom does not agree. Dung, after all, is mostly undigested food, and what is indigestible to a cow, for example, may be delightful to a beetle.

There are many different species of dung beetles, and they have various methods for gathering and storing their favorite food. Some simply grab little bits of dung and scurry away. Others quickly bury chunks of the stuff wherever they find it, to keep it away from rivals. But the dung beetles that so interested the Egyptians have a more elaborate routine. Using their jaws, forelegs, and their shovel-shaped head, these beetles cut, pat, and shape pieces of dung into a large ball. Then, walking backward, they roll the dung ball away from its original site to a spot where the soil is suitable for deep digging. There they excavate a large chamber in which they bury their treasure. These chambers can be quite big—some dung balls are the size of a softball.

The cleared-out chamber will become a nest for the beetle's eggs. When the eggs hatch, the newborn beetles will feed off the dung that their parents have so carefully provided.

To the ancient Egyptians, the actions of the beetles were very similar to those of the sun god, Ra. Just as the beetles rolled their ball of dung across the fields, so, every day, did Ra roll the ball of the sun across the sky. Just as the dung ball then disappeared below the Earth, so too did the sun sink from sight at night.

Some historians think that the Egyptians might have carried the parallel further. When, after several months, they saw new beetles emerge from the ground, they might have seen the beetles' appearance as mirroring the rebirth of their own dead in the afterlife. It is even possible that the Egyptians began their practice of building underground burial chambers by imitating the dung beetles digging out their nests. The very notion of turning their dead into mummies may have begun with the image of a beetle becoming a pupa—a cocoonlike stage the beetle goes through before it becomes an adult.

Certainly, the Egyptians displayed their sacred scarabs—a word that refers both to the dung beetles themselves and to carved images of them—everywhere. The beetles appeared as hieroglyphs, stone carvings, jewelry, and good luck symbols. Routinely, a carved beetle was placed on the chest of a mummy. Its purpose was to serve as a new heart (since the old one had been removed) that would accompany the soul of the dead on its journey to the afterlife.

Dung beetles influenced the cultures of other ancient people also. The Romans, after their empire engulfed Egypt, began wearing scarabs for good luck and protection. The ancient Greeks used beetle imagery, too, though not always so respectfully. They used the dung beetle as a character in stories and plays, but they most often focused on the comic potential of the beetle's preferred food.

ANCIENT EGYPTIANS SAW SUCH CLOSE SIMILARITIES BETWEEN THE DUNG BEETLE AND THE SUN GOD, RA, THAT THEY OFTEN PORTRAYED THE TWO AS ONE.

According to a medieval superstition, righting an upside-down beetle
would bring a person good luck.

Centuries later, during the Middle Ages, the beetle's reputation changed. Christian Europeans more and more associated scarabs with sin and the devil. To most people, dung beetles became things to be avoided.

Other beetles became linked with various superstitions. In medieval Germany, for example, killing a dor, or "witch," beetle brought bad luck. On the other hand, finding the beetle on its back and turning it over brought good luck. Throughout western Europe, stag beetles were always bad news—people thought the beetles carried burning coals in their huge, grasping jaws and set thatched roofs on fire. They also believed that stag beetles attracted lightning. Farther east, though, in Turkey, people wore the head and jaws of these same beetles as amulets to protect them against the evil eye.

Beetles pop up in the myths of peoples around the world. In South America, stories cast the dung beetle as the creator of the world and as the sculptor who fashioned the first men and women from clay. People in India and Indonesia devised similar myths.

These various appearances in folklore reflect a human fascination with Earth's most prevalent animal. The tales are part of a tradition that stretches back into the time before history. More than 24,000 years ago, Ice Age people in Europe were carving stone beetles. Exactly what these carvings were for, we do not know. But it is not much of a stretch to imagine that their creators saw the beetle as a link to divine powers.

2 A History of the Beetles

As members of the great class of insects, beetles can trace their history all the way back to the very first days of animal life on land. Insects first appeared on Earth around 400 million years ago, soon after a group of small sea creatures inched their way out of the water and onto dry land. These creatures were arthropods, a name that means "jointed legs." They had a body divided into segments, covered with a hard outer casing, and held up by legs that could bend in a great variety of combinations. Arthropods are easily the most common type of animal on the planet today, so the design was obviously a good one. It is shared by all the lobsters, crabs, shrimps, and similar creatures in the sea, and by all the millipedes, centipedes, spiders, scorpions, insects, and their kin on the land.

Over time, the land arthropods gradually changed, or evolved, and the insect groups we know today began to appear. Beetles were not the first. Tens of millions of years before the first

OVER MANY MILLIONS OF YEARS, BEETLES HAVE EVOLVED INTO A BEWILDERING VARIETY OF SHAPES AND SIZES. THESE EXTREMELY LONG FRONT LEGS BELONG TO A MALE SCARAB.

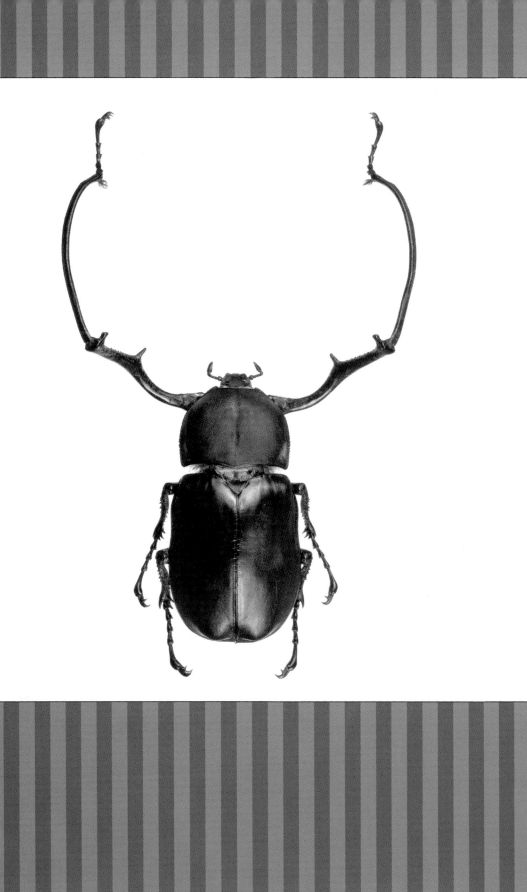

beetle walked onstage, Earth was filled with darting dragonflies and scuttling cockroaches. It took more than 100 million years of evolution before beetles showed up. But by 250 million years ago, the beetles had joined a grand parade of insect variety, taking their place alongside grasshoppers and crickets, lice and flies, bees and wasps and ants.

Remarkably, we can easily recognize even the earliest beetles, though they were somewhat different from their modern descendants—their armorlike outer wing covers were longer than they are in today's beetles, for example, and did not close as tightly. But their slightly flattened bodies were just like the bodies of beetles that today tunnel under the bark of trees. Those early beetles were most likely doing the same thing a couple of hundred million years ago, turning to trees as a perfect source of shelter and food.

Not *just* trees, though—at the time, insects of all sorts were exploiting plants of all sorts at every opportunity. In fact, the history of insects cannot be understood apart from the history of plants. The two go hand in hand—or at least, leaf in mouth. Plants and insects are an example of what scientists call coevolution—over time, changes in one group forced changes in the other, in a kind of back-and-forth struggle for survival. As insects devoured plants for food, plants developed ways of defending themselves. Some grew slippery, some became poisonous, some wrapped their seeds in tough cases. Insects responded in kind. They developed grasping feet and stronger jaws and became immune to the poisons.

No group of insects was better at battling the plants than the beetles. From the beginning, beetles were powerful eating machines. It was probably the beetles' gnashing jaws that pushed one group of trees (ancestors of today's pines, spruce, and other evergreens) to develop tough cones to cover their

THIS GREEN TORTOISE BEETLE MIMICS THE COLORING OF A LEAF IN A RAIN FOREST IN NORTHERN SOUTH AMERICA. BEETLES AND PLANTS HAVE ALWAYS BEEN ENGAGED IN BATTLE. HERE THE BEETLE APPEARS TO HAVE THE ADVANTAGE, EXPLOITING A LEAF FOR BOTH FOOD AND DISGUISE.

tender and nutritious seeds. To protect themselves against beetles that gnawed into their trunks, these same trees later developed a sticky sap, or resin, to stop the attackers in their six-footed tracks.

The Sticky Evidence

How do we know all this about beetles and plants of so long ago? Partly we have that sticky resin itself to thank. Over millions of years, the sap that oozed out of those ancient trees hardened

AMONG THE MANY ICE AGE ANIMALS TRAPPED IN THE LA BREA TAR PITS THOUSANDS
OF YEARS AGO WAS THIS BEETLE, A WATER-DWELLING SCAVENGER.

into a hard, yellowish, transparent substance called amber. Amber is a wonderful material, prized by jewelry makers who carve it into beautiful beads. But it is also prized by paleontologists—scientists who study the life of the distant past—because amber preserves anything trapped inside it. Today paleontologists have preserved in amber many nearly perfect specimens of beetles that were caught in the middle of eating one day tens of millions of years ago.

Amber is not the only stuff that wrapped up some ancient beetles so nicely for us. There are the more familiar fossil examples of beetles trapped in wet sand or mud that eventually hardened into rock. But rock-encased insects are not as easy to find as larger, bonier creatures are. Insects are too small and delicate, and generally their bodies are destroyed long before their final resting place turns to stone. Still, there are—and were—a great many beetles on Earth, and enough were buried in sediments to give us a good fossil record of their ancient history.

Beetles of the more recent past—"recent" in this case meaning the past 40,000 years or so—were also preserved in the famous La Brea tar pits in Los Angeles. The pits are spots where pools of sticky, natural asphalt, or tar, once formed. The tar was often covered by leaves and water, and many animals, stepping into the hidden tar accidentally, became trapped and died. Before their bodies slowly sank out of view, however, they attracted a crowd of insects that specialized in eating dead flesh. Among them were beetles, many of which also became trapped in the tar. Their outer bodies, along with the bones of the animals they fed on, have been preserved in the tar for hundreds of centuries.

Among the insects of La Brea were two species of dung beetles that are now extinct. These particular beetles had the misfortune to be specialists. They fed only on the dung of Ice Age mammals such as saber-toothed cats and ground sloths. When, at the end of the Ice Age, those mammals became extinct, the beetles that depended on them disappeared also.

Beetles Today

After more than 200 million years, beetles have achieved a success and a diversity unmatched by any other group of animals. Earth seems tailor-made for beetles, and one of science's most famous quotes points to this fact. A reporter once asked the

THE GOLDEN SCARAB IS JUST ONE OF THE UNTOLD THOUSANDS OF BEETLE SPECIES LIVING IN THE RAIN FORESTS OF CENTRAL AND SOUTH AMERICA.

great British biologist J. B. S. Haldane what he thought could be learned about God from a close study of life's creations. "An inordinate fondness for beetles," Haldane replied.

"Fondness" hardly begins to describe it. There are at least one and a half million species of animals on Earth. At least one million of them are insects. And at least one-third of all insects are beetles. It is necessary to keep repeating "at least" because the truth is that nobody knows precisely how many species of animals exist. Over the centuries, people have given names to around one and a half million, but no one knows how many species are still undiscovered. Thousands of new ones are being found every year. The huge majority of them are insects, and most of these are discovered in tropical rain forests.

It is certain that there are many, many thousands of beetle species we have never seen, living invisibly in the tops of rain forest trees or burrowing beneath the forest floor. There may be hundreds of thousands of species of these unknown beetles—no one really knows. Sadly, we will probably never know. Much of the rain forest is being destroyed by people hungry for land, and as the rain forest disappears, the beetles and other creatures that live there vanish along with it.

Scientists do not even know for sure how many beetle species we already know about. There are thousands upon thousands of beetle specimens lying in collections in natural history museums around the world, and no one has ever been able to make an accurate count of them all. A fair estimate is that between 300,000 and 350,000 beetle species have been named so far—that is, a *third of a million* distinct types of beetles.

For comparison, there are approximately 4,000 species of mammals, the large group of animals that includes elephants, tigers, bears, whales, horses, hippos, and humans. The beetles alone outnumber mammals by around eighty to one. Keep in mind that means eighty *species* of beetles for every species of mammals. In terms of individuals—well, that number is simply incalculable. There are a *lot* of individual beetles in the world.

3 Beetle Bodies

Although there are hundreds of thousands of beetle species, every one of them shares the same basic insect design. They all have soft bodies encased in a harder outer layer that functions like armor. This armor serves not only as the beetle's protective suit but also as its skeleton. The external skeleton, or exoskeleton, provides support for the beetle's body and allows it to stand upright, just as our own skeleton does. Attached to the inside of the exoskeleton are all the muscles that allow beetles to move their various parts—and with beetles, as with all insects, there are a fair number of parts to move.

The basic beetle body includes six legs, two antennae, four wings, two eyes, and an assembly of sometimes odd tools for biting and chewing. In addition, there are organs for breathing air, digesting food, pumping blood, eliminating wastes, and reproducing.

Like all insects, beetles are generally small, but that does not mean that they are uncomplicated. The beetle body is a marvelously complex machine that has been perfected over hundreds of millions of years. The exoskeleton, to start with, is made up of layers of protein and a substance called chitin.

A GIRAFFE WEEVIL DISPLAYS SOME OF THE EXTREME MODIFICATIONS MANY BEETLE SPECIES HAVE UNDERGONE.

Chitin is lightweight but tough, and it works well at both protecting beetles from hazards and letting them walk, run, climb, and fly. Also, unlike, say, a clamshell, an exoskeleton is not a single, smooth, continuous surface. Rather, it is a series of plates that together cover the entire body. The plates are sometimes quite complex in shape, and at places they dip or curve inward to provide attachment points for muscles and give the body additional support.

Like a suit of armor, an insect's exoskeleton has joints that allow the different sections to move. At the joints, the exoskeleton is thinner and more flexible. Also like armor, an insect's suit

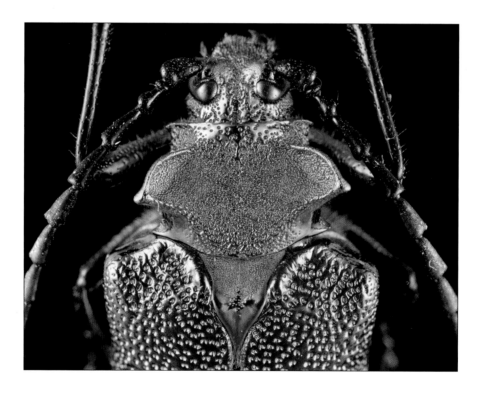

When magnified, an exoskeleton reveals the complex shape and texture that allows it to both support and protect an insect.

is thickest where the most protection is needed—on top of the head, for instance—and thinner over those spots less exposed to danger.

The exoskeleton protects against the environment as well as against predators. It is covered by a waxy film that keeps the body from drying out. At the same time, it has to allow oxygen to flow in, so it is pierced at a number of spots with air holes.

All in all, an exoskeleton is a perfectly wonderful framework for a body. But the design has one major drawback. Because the exoskeleton is stiff, it does not allow the body inside to grow larger. That is why at several times during its life an animal with an exoskeleton must molt, or shed its suit of armor, and grow a new one.

How to Build a Beetle

Because insects are designed so differently from mammals, it is sometimes hard for us to understand just how their bodies work. In some ways, an insect is very much like a toy made up of identical snap-together parts. An insect's body is composed of three major sections, and each section is made of ringlike units, or disks, that are strung together. These disks are the basic insect building blocks. A series of disks, from several to more than a dozen, form each of the three major parts of the insect's body: the head at the front, the thorax in the middle, and the abdomen at the rear.

The head, naturally, is where the beetle has its eyes and mouth and, inside, its brain. In addition the head sports two antennae, which are often nestled up against the eyes.

Many beetles also sport head ornaments that are commonly called horns, though they are really outgrowths of the exoskeleton. Horns come in a shocking variety of shapes and

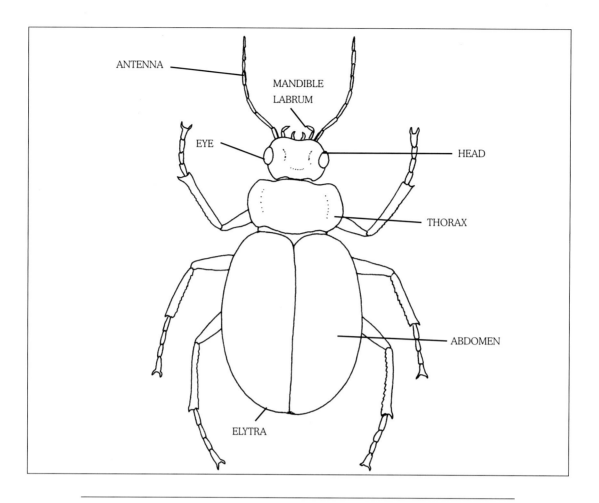

ANTENNA

MANDIBLE
LABRUM

EYE

HEAD

THORAX

ABDOMEN

ELYTRA

BEETLES, LIKE ALL INSECTS, ARE DIVIDED INTO THREE DISTINCT SECTIONS, WITH THE
MIDDLE SECTION, THE THORAX, BEARING THE LEGS AND WINGS.

arrangements, and they do not all sprout from the beetle's head. Some jut out from the thorax or from the front legs. Some look more like tusks than horns, and they can be straight or curved, long and slender, or short and thick. One of the most flamboyant examples is displayed by the large male Atlas beetles of Southeast Asia, which face the world with a set of headgear that would make any triceratops proud. Scientists do not know precisely what function these horns serve. But most think that the male beetles use their horns to grapple with other males when competing for mates. In other species, both male and female beetles have horns. The females apparently use theirs to fend off rivals for the best egg-laying spots.

The second section of the body, the thorax, is itself made of three main sections. They are called, from front to back, the prothorax, mesothorax, and metathorax. Each of these three sections has a pair of legs attached to it. The middle and rear sections also each have a pair of wings. This is the design not just for beetles, of course—it is how all insect bodies are arranged.

The third section, the abdomen, is the body's factory. The abdomen is where most of the machinery is housed for digesting food, getting rid of wastes, circulating blood, and producing eggs or sperm. Like the rest of the body, the abdomen is made up of individual segments; the number varies, but it is usually around ten.

Wings and Wing Covers

Most insects use all four of their wings to fly, but there are many that do not. Flies, for example, have extremely small front wings, which they use only to keep them steady during flight. Other insects, such as fleas, have gradually lost their wings altogether. Beetles have taken a different course. They have evolved forewings that act as hard shields to cover their back, and these give beetles their characteristic appearance.

Insect wings are made of a thin sandwich of chitin, the same material that forms the exoskeleton. In beetle wings, the beneficial qualities of chitin are on full display. The front, protective wings, called elytra, exploit chitin's toughness. The rear wings, used for flying, take advantage of its light weight. They are delicate and flexible, and when not in use they are folded up beneath the hard, thickened front wings.

These hardened wing covers are what make beetles look like the armored tanks of the insect world. When they are closed over the rear wings, the elytra meet in a straight line down

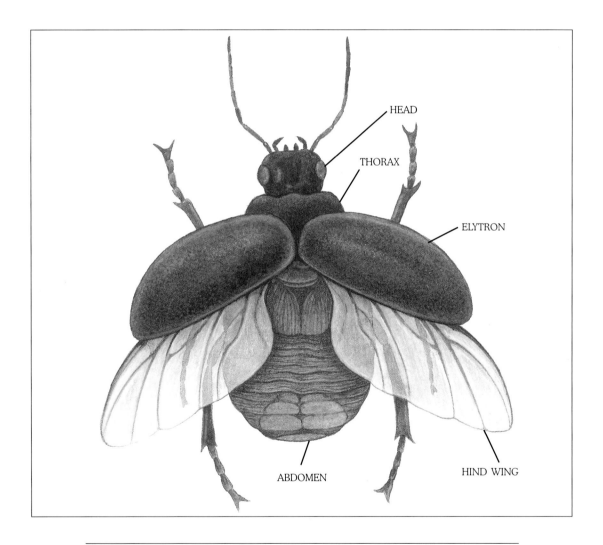

WITH ITS WING COVERS CLOSED, A BEETLE MAY APPEAR TO HAVE TWO PAIRS OF LEGS ATTACHED TO ITS ABDOMEN.

the middle of the beetle's back. In this position they cover up the middle and end sections of the thorax and, usually, all of the abdomen. (Seen from above, a beetle looks like its three main body sections are its head, its prothorax, and its elytra.)

The elytra are also what make many beetles such colorful characters. A great number of beetles have elytra that are decorated in a vivid array of colors and patterns—bright reds, yellows, oranges, blues, and greens, stippled with dots, slashed with zigzags, and tricked out with racing stripes. One of the most familiar examples is the common ladybug, with its bright red, black-dotted elytra. But the most spectacular examples belong to the group known as the jewel beetles. These elongated, streamlined beetles are decked out in bright metallic colors, and they are highly prized by beetle collectors.

Legs

Beetle legs, like other insect parts, are a string of connected parts. Most commonly, each leg has five segments, ending in a foot and, usually, a claw. Most beetles have six legs that are all more or less the same length. But many do not—over time, beetles have developed an enormous variety of leg shapes and sizes that have enabled them to dwell in different habitats and make use of different food sources.

Predators that race along the ground, such as the appropriately named tiger beetle, have long, thin legs. Persistent diggers, such as dung beetles, have short, thick legs. Some plant-dwelling beetles that must make their way from stem to stem may have greatly lengthened front legs, while others may have longer legs in the rear. Many climbing beetles have pads on their feet made of hundreds of very fine hairs. These hairs work like suction cups to allow the beetles to walk upside down on smooth surfaces. Desert-dwelling beetles often walk on long, stiltlike legs that keep their bodies as far as possible from blistering sands. Other beetles use flattened, paddle-like legs to swim through ponds and streams. Still others, with legs sprouting an assortment of pointed or shovel-like bumps, dig and burrow in forests and gardens.

Mouth

Nearly all beetles bite and chew. There are few delicate nectar-sippers or liquid lappers among them. Even the word *beetle* highlights this characteristic: it comes from the Old English word *bitan*, meaning "to bite." Naturally, the structure of the various parts that make up the beetle's mouth reflects this preference for chomping.

Beetles have two pairs of jaws—called mandibles and maxillae—for grabbing, ripping, and grinding their food. The mandibles are in front, and they are always the larger pair. In many beetles the mandibles are very large indeed, and sometimes they curve inward like a scythe or scimitar. Rows of pointed "teeth"—hard, sharp peaks of chitin—often line the mandibles, making them even more menacing. Beetles equipped with such jaws are essentially walking around with a pair of steak knives in front of their face. In the great majority of beetles, these jaws come together from the sides, though in some they close vertically, as ours do.

Once the mandibles have seized something edible, the second set of jaws, the maxillae, move the food into the mouth. Usually the maxillae are assisted by a pair of delicate, very mobile "fingers"—they actually look like small, extra legs—called palps. The whole assembly of jaws and palps is then covered by an upper lip, called a labrum, and protected underneath by a lower lip, called a labium.

This, at any rate, is the general mouth plan, but there are as many variations in the shape and size of beetle mouthparts as there are different kinds of beetle. Some groups do without certain parts entirely. Pesky, crop-eating weevils, for example, have their mouth perched on the end of a long snout—the better to get into seeds and stems—and have dispensed with the labrum completely. Stag beetles have mandibles that may be half as long as the rest of their body and are so toothed and branched that they look like the antlers of a deer.

Muscles and Locomotion

Like all animals, beetles use a complex set of muscles to make their way through the world. Throughout the body these muscles are attached to the inside of the exoskeleton.

EQUIPPED WITH POWERFUL TOOTHED JAWS FOR GRABBING AND TEARING APART PREY, A TIGER BEETLE IS A FEROCIOUS HUNTER OF OTHER INSECTS.

The muscles at the front end of the beetle are dedicated chiefly to the serious business of eating, with most allocated to the large, powerful mandibles. At the back end, in the abdomen, muscles power the machinery of the circulatory, digestive, and reproductive systems. Meanwhile, in the middle, the muscles of the thorax drive the ten appendages—the legs and wings—that a beetle needs to get its front end to food and its back end to mates and suitable egg-laying sites.

Legs and, especially, wings take an enormous amount of power and coordination—if you are chasing after a meal or trying to avoid becoming one, it is not wise to be tripping over your own six feet or crashing into a tree. Most beetles are sturdy walkers, and a fair number—generally predators—are fast runners as well.

Many beetles also use their legs for a host of other strenuous activities. They may depend on leg power for digging through soil or burrowing under bark, for lifting and moving dead prey, for swimming and diving, or, famously, for rolling huge balls of dung.

Like all other insects, beetles move their six legs in groups of three: the front and back leg on one side move together with the middle leg on the opposite side; then the other three legs move as a group. This tripod arrangement ensures that they always have a stabilizing three feet on the ground and so are not easily tipped over.

Because beetles use only two wings to fly instead of four, wing coordination poses less of a problem. Still, there is a complicated series of maneuvers that a beetle must go through. When closed, a beetle's elytra—the wing covers—lock together like floorboards: a "tongue" on one edge fits inside a groove on the other. So before a beetle can take to the air it must unlock

WHILE AIRBORNE, A LADYBUG MUST KEEP ITS ELYTRA OUT OF THE WAY OF ITS DELICATE FLIGHT WINGS (COLORED WHITE IN THE PHOTO).

its elytra. It does this by pulling the chitin plate that covers the middle section of its thorax down and slightly forward. This spreads the elytra outward, and they pop open, allowing the delicate wings beneath them to unfold. Those flight wings are often folded in complex ways. Generally, the tip of the wing is folded in, then the outer third is folded under or over the inner two thirds. Interestingly, the wings are not opened by muscle power. Between the two layers of chitin that make up the wing is a network of thin hollow tubes that fill with air to stiffen the wing.

Once the wing covers are opened, they usually lock in place, out of the way of the beating wings. Many beetles do use their elytra somewhat to help them fly. Some tilt the elytra up and forward, so that they act like airplane wings to give them additional lift as the air rushes underneath. A few beetle species—heavy rhinoceros beetles among them—actually flap their elytra a little in concert with their flying wings. (As one might expect, a flying rhinoceros needs all the help it can get.)

Beetles are usually strong fliers, but they are not graceful or speedy ones. The slow flight of an easily catchable ladybug or firefly is typical. In the air, beetles look very much like tanks outfitted with wings. At best, the smaller beetles get their wings moving at about 200 beats a second, which is not all that rapid compared with many other insects. But beetles do not generally require great flight speed or acrobatic aerial skills. They just need their wings to get them to food, to escape from danger, and to find mates. For these needs, their flying abilities prove more than adequate.

Circulation and Respiration

To keep their muscles moving, beetles need a constant supply of air and fuel, just as we do. But the insect system for circulating oxygen and blood is very different from our own. To start with, insects use two separate systems instead of one: their blood carries nutrients from food to all the cells in the body, as ours does, but it carries no oxygen. Nor do any insects have lungs for taking in oxygen. Rather, all insects, beetles included, use a much simpler method of air supply. They have a series of valves, called spiracles, on the outside of their body that open to allow air to flow in. In beetles, one pair of spiracles is located between the first and second sections of the thorax, and another pair is between the second and third sections. Up to eight more pairs are dotted along the abdomen. Each spiracle is connected to an air tube, called a trachea, that divides into thinner and thinner branches as it winds through the body's interior. Air flows through these tubes (tracheae) to supply oxygen directly to all the body's tissues.

The blood, meanwhile, is pumped by a heart—or more accurately, by several hearts. The beetle heart is made up of a series of muscular sacs in a long tube that runs beneath the exoskeleton along the beetle's back. Blood (technically called hemolymph) enters the heart through holes in the rear of the tube and is pumped forward toward the head. There, rather than progressing through an ever-finer system of arteries and capillaries, it simply spills out into the body's interior. This kind of circulatory system is known as an open system, as opposed to our own closed system in which the blood is always contained within blood vessels. In insects, the spilled pool of blood simply

THE COLORADO POTATO BEETLE HAS A HIGHLY EFFICIENT DIGESTIVE SYSTEM AND A HEARTY APPETITE; BOTH LARVAE AND ADULTS FEED ON PLANT LEAVES.

washes over the body's organs and tissues as it gradually makes its way back to the rear of the abdomen, where it picks up nutrients and flows again into the heart.

Digestion

Like its circulatory system, a beetle's digestive system is straightforward, and highly efficient. Although beetles have evolved in far greater variety than any other animal group, and although they eat a staggering array of different foods, they all share the same basic design for breaking down food and extracting nutrients. Essentially the digestive system is another long tube, running from the mouth, where food goes in, to the anus, where waste goes out. The system is made up of three parts, called the foregut, the midgut, and the hindgut. The purpose of each is to reduce bulky food into smaller and smaller bits.

This food disassembly line starts with the beetle's mighty jaws, which typically tear, rip, gnash, and gnaw at whatever edible item the beetle has a particular fondness for. Those chunks of food travel through the esophagus, in the foregut, to the crop, a kind of storage chamber where food may be partially digested. At the back of the foregut is the gizzard, an area of the tube lined with chitinous teeth and surrounded by muscle. Contractions of the muscle let the gizzard crunch and grind the food into smaller pieces, which are then passed into the midgut. There, digestive fluids dissolve the pieces into tiny particles. These continue on to the hindgut, which is where the blood picks up most of its supply of nutrients. The hindgut is also where most of the water from food is absorbed. Whatever is left eventually travels to the rectum, at the end of the hindgut, where the waste is packed into a dry pellet. It is worth noting that beetles have been the

During mating, a male *Eupholus* weevil from Papua New Guinea transfers sperm to a female, which will use it to fertilize her eggs.

subject of human interest for so long that we actually have a word, *frass*, that specifically refers to beetle feces.

Reproduction

Male beetles produce sperm in organs called testes, and females produce eggs in ovaries. Generally, sperm and eggs must be brought together so that the eggs can be fertilized and start to develop into beetle larvae. The number of eggs a female lays varies greatly with the species. Some short-lived beetles lay hundreds of eggs at a time. Some longer-lived beetles lay only a few.

Not all beetles follow the normal method of reproduction, however. In some beetle species, the females have found males to be an unnecessary complication in the business of producing babies. So they have simply gotten rid of them. In these species, a female's eggs develop into larvae without any fertilization by a male's sperm. The offspring are all copies, or clones, of the female. Many species of weevils, for example, reproduce in this way and so are represented only (or nearly only) by females.

Nervous System and Senses

Even the smallest beetle has room in its head for a brain; and although a beetle brain is certainly not large, it is big enough to do the job required.

An insect brain is not built to think deep thoughts. Its function is to process information that comes in through the senses and then to direct the many body parts to respond appropriately. Just as the body itself is divided into sections, so is the brain. One section receives information from the eyes, another from the antennae, and yet another from the labrum (the upper lip). Stretching from the brain and running along the insect's "belly" are its two main nerve cords. A series of bulges along the cords, formed by clusters of nerve cells, make up the rest of the beetle's central nervous system. These bulges, called ganglia, control activity in specific parts of the beetle. One pair of ganglia, for instance, right behind the brain, controls the mouthparts. Ganglia in the thorax control the wings. Other ganglia direct the legs, and still others, in the abdomen, manage the organs of digestion and reproduction. In effect, the brain of a beetle is divided among all these ganglia.

The sense organs are the brain's links to the outside world. Among them are the eyes and antennae.

As a rule, beetles are not intensely visual creatures. The need for sharp eyesight varies among the hundreds of thousands of beetle species, of course. Hunters need better vision than plant eaters, and beetles that live in dark caves rely less on their eyes than beetles that live in bright treetops. But even the sharpest-sighted beetle sees far less well than, say, a dragonfly.

Insects have compound eyes, which means that each eye is made up of many individual, usually hexagon-shaped, units. The number of units, or facets, in an insect's eye tells us how much the insect depends on its sight. Fast, predatory dragonflies, for example, may have 30,000 facets in each eye. Most beetles, in contrast, have no more than a few hundred. Some flightless beetles have only a few dozen facets per eye, and some cave dwellers have no eyes at all.

Most other insects also have on their head a trio of extra, simple eyes, called ocelli. Ocelli are not fully functioning eyes—they do not form images—but they do detect light and dark. Among beetles, though, ocelli are rare.

Beetles can see colors, and many probably see infrared and ultraviolet light as well—light that is invisible to us unless we are using some high-tech device, such as night-vision goggles. But sight is not the primary sense for most beetles. There are exceptions—most notably the fireflies, or lightning bugs, which have to spot a potential mate's flashing light from far away. In general, though, beetles can see objects that are no more than five or six inches (12 to 15 cm) away, unless the object is very large and moving. The hundreds of facets in each eye do not form a complete image of whatever is in front of them. Rather, each facet sees only a small part of the scene. The many parts are probably not put together by the beetle's brain to form one coherent image. What the beetle really registers, without thought, is any change in the image caused by movement.

Most beetles rely on some sense other than sight, but that sense is not so easy for us to understand. Think of it as a combination of taste, touch, and smell. Some of this sensory information is provided by fine hairs, studded with sensors, that bristle from a beetle's legs and palps. These hairs allow the beetle to distinguish the four basic tastes—sweet, salty, bitter, and acidic—just as our tastebuds do. But the beetle's chief sense organs are the antennae.

A beetle's antennae are able to detect faint vibrations; gauge humidity, air pressure and temperature; and receive invisible chemical messages floating through the air. With their remarkable antennae, beetles can find food and water, sense the approach of predators, and communicate with other members of their species.

Beetle antennae come in a dizzying variety of shapes and sizes. Most antennae have eleven segments, but some have more and others fewer. The long-horned wood-boring beetles have the longest. They sport slender, waving, hairlike antennae that are often as long as the rest of their body and sometimes two or even three times as long. Other beetle antennae are short and club shaped, while still others may be twisted, bent, saw-toothed, flattened, delicately spread out like a feather, or punctuated like a string of beads. The shape of the antennae often gives a clue to their primary purpose. Feathery antennae, for example, usually indicate that the beetle has an increased ability to sense pheromones, or chemical signals, released by another beetle looking for a mate.

Because their antennae are so important, beetles always keep them free of dust and dirt that could clog up their delicate sensors. For cleaning, most beetles use their mandibles. Some, though, have special grooves in their front legs, through which they pull their antennae to wipe them off.

Some beetles use their antennae to hear. Unlike grasshoppers or crickets or other noisy insects, most beetles do not have anything like ears. But many have antennae that are especially sensitive to sound vibrations. By rubbing various body parts against each other, those beetles make sounds that their fellow beetles can detect.

A few beetle types, including tiger beetles, have developed ears of a sort: a thin membrane that vibrates, like an eardrum, in response to sounds. In tiger beetles these ears are located on the sides of the body at the very front of the abdomen. They appear to be sensitive only to extremely high-pitched sounds, such as those made by echolocating bats, well beyond the range of human hearing.

4   Life Cycle

Most beetles are secretive creatures. They prefer to stay out of view, away from the attention of predators. Even the most familiar beetles are animals we see only as adults, after they have acquired their wings and their characteristic colors and markings. But the adult stage of a beetle's life is usually rather short. The longer, preceding stages are likely to pass without our notice.

Beetles, like many insects, go through four stages in life: egg, larva, pupa, and adult. Their process of growth is called complete metamorphosis. Like butterflies, they change their bodies dramatically as they mature.

When a beetle emerges from its egg, it looks little like the insect it will, with luck, become. Beetle larvae—often called grubs—do not appear as miniature beetles. They more closely resemble worms, or miniature lizards. They do not have an adult's wings, and they may not have legs able to get them from one spot to another. But they usually do have biting mouthparts that are ready to start eating.

A LILY BEETLE LAYS HER EGGS ON A LILY LEAF, GUARANTEEING THAT THE LARVAE WILL HATCH ATOP THE FOOD THEY NEED.

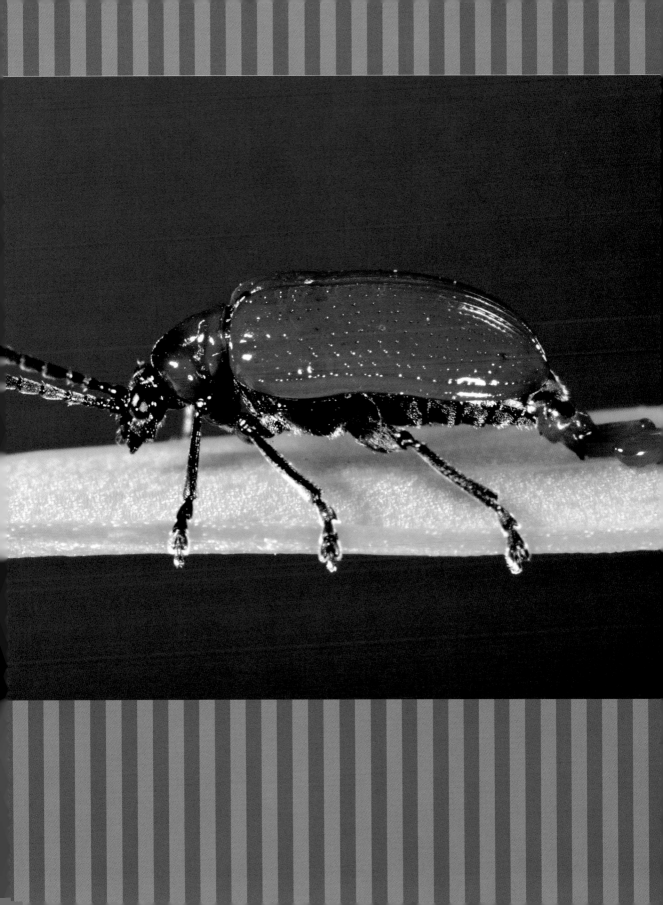

Grubs are essentially eating machines. A grub's job is to grow quickly, and it accomplishes this task by eating as much as it can. What a grub eats depends on what kind of beetle it is, and a grub's body mirrors its needs. Grubs that are active hunters—ladybug grubs, for instance, which feed on aphids— have fully working legs and strong jaws. Beetle larvae that feed on plant roots or buried food have legs built for grabbing and holding on, not for moving. Other body parts, such as antennae, may be simpler than they are in adults or missing altogether. Grubs have no wings or sexual organs, and they often have two to six simple ocelli rather than two compound eyes.

As the grub grows, it eventually becomes too big for its skin. When this point is reached, the larva must molt—it breaks out of its exoskeleton, throws it away, and grows a new one. The number of times it has to molt depends on the species. Most beetles molt between three and fourteen times, over a period of a few weeks to few months. A few beetles go through as many as twenty-nine molts. Others seem never to want to grow up. June beetles spend as long as five years underground, slowly growing.

After a beetle larva has molted for the last time, it becomes a pupa. At this stage, it is just beginning to look like an adult. The pupa usually has visible wings, but they look more like small pads than the intricate wings of a mature beetle. It does not have a grown-up's armor either. The pupa's body is softer than an adult's, and it is usually not as colorful.

The pupal stage is the beetle's most secretive. After their last molt, beetle larvae stop eating. Those that are already below ground stay put. Those that are above ground, though, feeding on plants, usually drop to the surface and begin to burrow. Water-dwelling beetle larvae may dig into soft mud lining the shore. Insect-hunting ground beetle grubs burrow beneath rocks or under fallen leaves.

What all these grubs are seeking is protection—during their pupal stage, they are especially vulnerable to predators, and so they try to get out of sight. They are also seeking spots where they can enjoy fairly steady temperatures and humidity. The specific needs vary. Some beetle larvae burrow only 6 inches (15 cm) underground. Others dig down a few feet.

Not all beetles follow this pattern. Wood-boring beetle larvae dig a tunnel beneath the surface of a tree trunk. Ladybugs are unusual in that they stay out in the open. A ladybug grub is essentially shaped like half a sphere. When it enters the pupal stage, it cements its flat side to the surface of a leaf. The rounded top side is camouflaged for protection. Before they take on their familiar red, black-dotted appearance, ladybugs look remarkably like bird droppings. Apparently, this makes them less than appealing to most predators.

Few beetles actually weave cocoons. They just go into a resting state while their new bodies are forming beneath their skin. But because most beetles go through their pupal stage underground or hidden, the change from larva to adult is a process we rarely get to see. It may last anywhere from a few days to a few months, depending on the species and the climate. When the adult body has finally formed, the beetle emerges with its new armor strong and hard, its wings ready to unfold, its antennae ready to receive messages. It has all the equipment it needs to embark on its next, most important mission: to make more beetles.

Finding a Mate

Beetles of all varieties populate the Earth by the billions and trillions. So one might think that for any particular beetle, finding a mate would not be much of a challenge. Indeed, for some

BENEATH A TREE'S BARK, THE LARVAE OF BARK BEETLES EAT AND GROW WITHIN A COMPLEX SERIES OF INTERCONNECTING TUNNELS.

beetles it is not. For many others, however, finding the right male or female takes some doing.

Beetles that have the easiest time of it are those that live in large numbers on a shared food source, such as the leaves of a single tree. Males and females of these beetles can depend on just bumping into each other when the time is right. They do not need to employ any elaborate mate-finding techniques.

Other beetles, though, living more solitary lives, cannot afford to wait until that special one-in-a-billion beetle just happens to trundle by. These beetles need to advertise their availability.

Beetles have a few dependable methods of calling out to members of the opposite sex. The first is sound. Many bark beetles, long-horned beetles, and bess beetles produce a wide range of raspy calls. In fact, bess beetles (they are also called betsy beetles, patent leather beetles, peg beetles, and many other names) probably make a greater variety of sounds than any other insect, frog, or toad. They even outdo most birds.

Bess beetles speak by rubbing their wings, which are lined with ridges, over their back. This rubbing—called stridulation—makes a sound like that of a file grating against a piece of wood. The beetles' energetic melodies may not sound pleasant to human ears, but to other beetles they are heavenly. Future mates, captivated by the sounds they "hear" through their antennae, crawl or fly over to meet the musician of their dreams.

Other beetles have more unusual noisemaking strategies. South African tok-tokkies thump their abdomens against the ground. Female death-watch beetles, which like to live inside the floors, walls, and furniture of human homes, literally beat their heads against the walls of their chewed-out tunnels to attract the attention of males. The knocking sounds have persuaded many startled people that their home is inhabited by something more ghostly than a small dark beetle looking for love.

Pheromones—chemical signals similar to odors—allow for more subtle advertising. Once released, they are akin to beetle perfume wafting long distances through the air. The pheromones have a powerful effect on other beetles of the same species, which can detect the signals even when they are very faint.

Diamonds in the Sky

The flashiest mating method, though, belongs to the beetles that advertise with light. Fireflies, or lightning bugs, are easily the best-known examples, but they are not the only ones. There are actually three different families of light-producing beetles—click

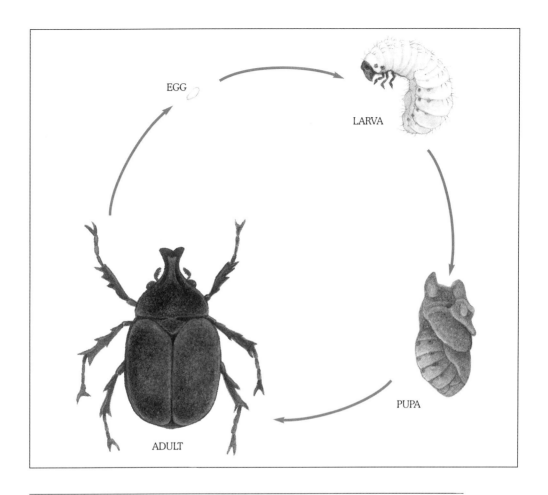

MOST BEETLES GO THROUGH COMPLETE METAMORPHOSIS, A LIFE CYCLE THAT INVOLVES FOUR DISTINCT STAGES: EGG, LARVA, PUPA, AND ADULT.

beetles and glowworms make up the other two—and they include thousands of beetle species.

These beetles are definitely among the leading lights of the insect class. Bioluminescence—an organism's ability to produce light—is a complicated and impressive process. It involves several different chemicals, interacting in many thousands of cells in the beetle's body. The result is a light that gives off virtually no heat whatsoever—a tremendous achievement, compared to a light bulb.

The ways beetles use their light to communicate is just as complex. Different firefly species produce light that ranges in color from light green to yellow to orange to pale red. Each species also flashes its lights in its own distinctive code, a series of off-and-on blinks at specific intervals. Usually, it is the male that flies around slowly, spelling out his name (well, at least his species name) in flashing lights. The female, perched on a leaf or a blade of grass, must pick out a male with the right color light flashing in the right sequence, with each "on" and each "off" lasting exactly the right amount of time. When she does, she responds with coded flashes of her own, and the male homes in on her signal.

The most spectacular light displays are known as firefly trees, and they occur in parts of Asia when huge numbers of a single firefly species gather in a single tree. At first the males all follow their own individual promptings, and the tree twinkles with the blinks of thousands of lights. But soon the beetles begin to adjust their flashing until they are all in sync—thousands of fireflies blinking on and off, on and off, in unison.

Preparing for the Next Generation

Once an adult male and female beetle meet, the goal is always the same: to produce offspring. The male climbs onto the female's back, and through his reproductive organ, transfers sperm to her body. Afterward, the female beetle stores the sperm in a compartment called a spermatheca. She may keep the sperm there for days or weeks, or even as long as several months. Not until she lays her eggs are the eggs mixed with the sperm and fertilized.

THIS TORTOISE BEETLE BELONGS TO THE MINORITY OF BEETLE SPECIES THAT STAY WITH THEIR EGGS AND PROTECT THEIR YOUNG AFTER HATCHING.

After mating, most male beetles (though there are some exceptions) leave, playing no active role in ensuring the survival of the next generation. To the extent that beetles provide any help to their offspring, it is the female's job.

Females of a few beetle species lay their eggs anywhere. The chances that any one of those eggs will survive are poor, but the beetle lays so many eggs that it is certain that at least some will succeed. The great majority of beetles, however, take some care in selecting a spot for the eggs that will provide the hatched larvae with sufficient food.

Leaf-eating beetles, for example, glue their eggs to a suitably edible leaf or stem. Ladybugs make sure that their little grubs will hatch on a plant crawling with the slow-moving aphids they find so delicious. Bark beetles ease their eggs under the bark of a tree, and soil-dwelling beetles tuck their future offspring under rocks or beneath a blanket of dead leaves.

A few beetles provide additional help for their eggs, besides simply choosing the right neighborhood for them. Some tortoise beetles (a glance at their rounded backs and circular outlines reveals the origin of their name) cover their eggs with a protective froth. The silver water beetle weaves a silk cocoonlike egg case, which it glues to a leaf it finds floating on the surface of the water. Other water beetles also spin silk cases, but they carry the cases around with them rather than risk abandoning them on a floating nursery.

Offering even more care are those beetles that create a heavily protected nest for their eggs and stock it with food. Some dig out elaborate tunnels in sand or mud. Ambrosia beetles bore out a nesting tunnel in a tree trunk, then fill it with nutritious fungi they have collected. Some plant-eating beetles likewise fill underground nests with decaying leaves or fruit.

Finally, there are those beetles that not only provide their offspring with a safe, well-stocked home, they also stick around to make sure that the grubs get off to a good start in life. Among these beetles are the dung eaters, the carrion eaters, and some of the leaf-eating tortoise beetles mentioned above, which shield their young with the flared edge of their "shell." By far, the best parents among the beetles are the carrion-eating burying beetles. In their safe, warm underground chamber, both the female and the male beetle watch over the eggs until they hatch. Then the parents help feed the larvae. Not until the grubs enter their pupal stage do the parents leave.

It is important to remember that this seemingly motherly behavior is no better than that of any other beetle species. What works best for one kind of animal is not necessarily what works best for another. Generally, the amount of care a beetle gives its eggs is related to the number of eggs it lays in the first place. Beetles that drop their eggs anywhere and move on lay hundreds or even thousands of eggs at a time. Beetles that lavish time and effort on their young, such as the burying beetles, may lay only a few eggs or even a single one. Both extreme strategies, and all the ones in between, are the means these beetles have evolved to make sure that at least some of their offspring survive.

Survival: Weaponry and Defenses

The odds against any individual beetle's survival are great. Beetles are constantly preyed on by a great army of predators. Among them are birds of all kinds, mammals large and small, lizards, spiders, fish, and of course, other insects. Were it not for the many defenses beetles have evolved over the eons, virtually none of them would live long enough to reproduce.

When threatened, most beetles immediately respond by flying or running away. Many times, though, a beetle is safe enough simply sitting still. Even among insects, a beetle's exoskeleton is unusually thick and strong. Against many small predators, a beetle's best defense strategy is to flatten itself against the ground or a tree trunk and rely on its armored exterior for protection. A number of beetles add another layer of protection by playing dead when threatened. Some even fall to the ground and lie on their back. The trick works, so long as the attacker will pursue only moving food.

Other beetles put off predators by being foul tasting. Ladybugs are among this group, and they rely on their undesirability to protect them even when they are most vulnerable: during the winter, when they go into hibernation. They gather by the thousands, snuggle together as tightly as possible, and then release a substance that predators find repellant. The amount of the foul-tasting stuff produced by each individual ladybug is small, but the total from the group is powerful enough to keep them all safe until spring.

Larger beetles are often equipped for mounting a more active defense and fighting back if necessary. Horns, strong legs, and most importantly, strong jaws are serious obstacles to all but the most determined diners. Of course, even for these beetles, it is far better to avoid attack in the first place, and many have developed a variety of ways to keep predators at a distance.

The first way is by camouflage. The color and texture of many beetle bodies often allow them to blend in with a background of leaves or bark. An equally large number of beetles, it seems, are designed not to blend in but to stand out. But these beetles have a taste for the tasteless—to the eyes of a predator, they look convincingly like the inedible droppings of insects, birds, or lizards.

A second effective mode of trickery is to look like another, more dangerous insect. Long-horned beetles are particularly skilled at this. Many members of that family have evolved to look like stinging bees or wasps. Others have developed forms that let them imitate acid-filled ants. Still others disguise themselves as distantly related beetles that are either poisonous or downright foul tasting. The off-putting relatives they mimic generally belong to one of three families: the blister beetles, the ground beetles, or the darkling beetles. All these groups make sophisticated use of chemical weapons.

Blister beetles produce a chemical called cantharidin, which is extremely irritating to the skin of most animals. Humans who incautiously handle blister beetles often end up with raw, blistered hands or arms. Humans who incautiously *eat* blister beetles could end up dead—cantharidin is highly poisonous.

Many ground beetles try to keep predators at a greater distance. In specialized chambers in their abdomen, they produce burning liquids that they spray, through an opening in their rear, at any animal that dares to bother them. Among the most notorious of these rear-gunners is the bombardier beetle. It has a very mobile nozzle at its rear end and an impressive aim. The bombardier's burning brew is made up of several separate chemicals that, when brought together, heat up to an alarming degree—212 degrees F (100° C). At that boiling temperature, the liquid turns into a gassy vapor that explodes out of the beetle's end with a popping sound easily heard by any human foolish or brave enough to be within range.

A similar weapon-at-the-rear strategy is used by the family of darkling beetles. One well-known family member is the pinacate beetle, a resident of the American Southwest that more commonly goes by the name of the stinkbug beetle. Its defense consists of raising its rear high into the air and firing off a spray that quickly sends most attackers fleeing in the opposite direction. Not all predators are deterred, though. The grasshopper mouse has developed an ingenious attack strategy of its own. Upon finding a stinkbug beetle, the mouse grabs it with its paws, rams its dangerous back end into the ground, and eats its more delectable front end.

Other chemical-carrying beetles do not produce deadly substances themselves but acquire them by eating poisonous plants. Some beetles, for example, feed on milkweed. Like the larvae of the monarch butterfly, they store the milkweed's toxic chemicals in their body and thereby make themselves unappealing as food. Still other beetles do not produce or acquire any toxic substances but manage to make predators avoid them all the same. Through body shape or bright colors that often serve as warning signals to predators, they look similar enough to their poisonous cousins to share their reputation, even though the mimics themselves are harmless. In the beetle world, sometimes looking dangerous is as good as being dangerous.

5 Meet the Beetles

To make sense of the great variety of life found on Earth, scientists organize species into groups. All animals, for example, are divided up into broad categories called phyla (singular, *phylum*), based on their fundamental design. Beetles, along with all other insects, arachnids (spiders, scorpions, and their kin), millipedes, centipedes, and crustaceans (lobsters, crabs, shrimp, etc.), are in the phylum Arthropoda. Each phylum is then divided into the smaller and smaller groups known as class, order, family, genus, and finally, species.

All insects belong to the class Insecta. All beetles belong to the order Coleoptera, a name coined by the ancient Greek philosopher Aristotle. It comes from two words meaning "sheath" and "wings," and it refers to the beetles' characteristic wing covers. After that, classifying beetles can get complicated.

Coleopterists—scientists who specialize in studying beetles—do not all agree on just how many different families of beetles there are. But it is fair to say that there are more than 150. One widely accepted list includes 166. Some beetle families are small, with just a relative handful of species. Others are huge. The largest is the family of snout-nosed weevils (Curculionidae),

DESPITE THEIR GREAT DIVERSITY, BEETLES SHARE A FEW KEY FEATURES, SUCH AS THE WING COVERS THAT MEET IN A STRAIGHT LINE DOWN THE MIDDLE OF THEIR BACK.

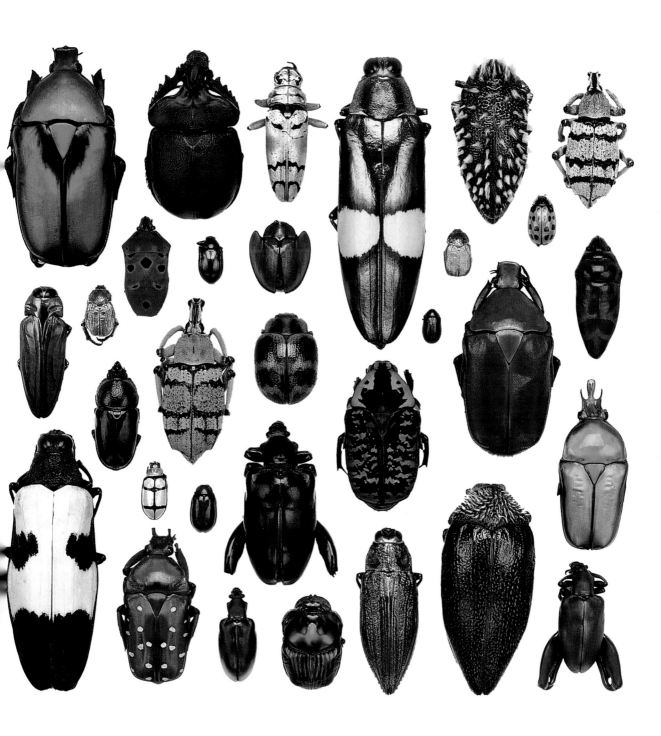

a motley group of plant and crop eaters; it contains more than 50,000 beetle species. Again for comparison, there are only some 9,000 different living birds of all types, from tiny hummingbirds to giant ostriches. Weevil species alone outnumber bird species by more than five to one.

Although there are a great number of beetle families, about two-thirds of all beetle species belong to just eight of them. Here are the eight biggest, with some intriguing representatives.

Jewel Beetles (family Buprestidae)

When these beetles make the transition from larva to adult, they get, in addition to a number of new body parts, a new name. They go from being "flat-headed wood borers" to "metallic wood borers" or, quite often, "jewels." As their early name indicates, these beetles are fond of trees, and they can be serious pests. The bronze birch borer, for example, kills birch trees by drilling (or "boring") tunnels beneath the bark, all around the tree. So the presence of buprestid larvae is definitely not a good thing for gardeners, homeowners, and caretakers of public parks.

As adults, however, many of these beetles become highly desirable to collectors because of the insects' brilliant, shining, metallic colors. Like custom-painted sports cars, jewel beetles' smooth oval bodies glisten with metallic greens, blues, yellows, oranges, reds, silver, and gold. Often these beetles are iridescent—their colors shift from one to another, depending on how the light hits them.

One of the oldest and most spectacular testaments to the allure of jewel beetles comes from Japan. There, in the seventh century, an empress had a shrine built to hold sacred Buddhist objects. The objects were decorated with more than 9,000 shining green beetle wings, set in gold.

THE SHINY METALLIC BODIES OF JEWEL BEETLES MAKE THEM DESIRABLE TO BOTH
BEETLE COLLECTORS AND MAKERS OF BEETLE JEWELRY.

Ground Beetles (family Carabidae)

This is a family of fierce hunters, and there are a lot of them—
more than 40,000 species. These predators are known as
ground beetles for the simple reason that the ground is where
most of them do their hunting. Many are very fast. One of the
fastest insects in the world is a member of this family: the
Australian tiger beetle, *Cicindela hudsoni*, a ferocious hunter that
can sprint along the forest floor at speeds of 8.2 feet (2.5 m) per
second. If that does not seem impressive enough, consider that
the beetle is only about .8 inch (20 mm) long, which means that

it is moving 120 times the length of its body each second. An equivalent speed for a six-foot (1.8-m) human would be 493 miles per hour (795 kph).

These hunters come equipped with vicious saw-toothed or scythe-shaped jaws for ripping apart their prey. Usually that prey consists of other insects, but not always. Some ground beetles specialize in snails.

Even the larvae of some ground beetles are ferocious, though they do not yet have the racing legs of the adults. Tiger beetle grubs, for example, rely on ambush. They hide in a vertical tunnel they dig into the soil, with their head poking just over the top. When an insect blunders by, the grub darts halfway out of the tunnel, grabs the prey in its sickle-shaped jaws, then drags it back inside.

All the ground beetles are nocturnal—that is, they are active only at night—and they instantaneously run and hide if exposed to light. Because they live in darkness, they are generally not brightly colored or marked with elaborate patterns. But there are exceptions, such as some shiny green tiger beetles and the flashy metallic-blue and green gypsy-moth hunter, which hunts down and devours impressive numbers of gypsy moth caterpillars. This beetle belongs to a group of caterpillar specialists, many of which turn out to be brightly colored as well. They also differ from other ground beetles in that they leave the ground, climbing up trees in pursuit of a caterpillar snack.

Long-horned Beetles (family Cerambycidae)

The long-horned beetles make up another family of tree borers, and with 25,000 to 30,000 species, it is among the most successful. A little confusingly, these beetles are named not for any hard chitin horns poking out of their heads but for their extremely long, waving antennae. For most of the family, these long antennae are a mark of their sensitivity to the world around them. They are ready to pick up any slight chemical messages or odors floating by. For at least one long-horn (*Hammaticherus batus*), though, the antennae are also weapons. This beetle's antennae are tipped with barbed spines. If attacked, the beetle turns its antennae into punishing whips that can rip open a predator's skin.

Another family member, the Asian long-horned beetle, has become infamous in the United States after first showing up in

DESPITE ITS ENORMOUS SIZE, *TITANUS GIGANTEUS* IS NOT EASY TO FIND, AND SCIENTISTS KNOW LITTLE ABOUT ITS LIFE IN SOUTH AMERICA'S RAIN FORESTS.

Brooklyn, New York, in 1996. The larvae of these beetles can destroy many kinds of trees, including maples, birches, and willows. Once they have gotten into a tree, there is no way to stop their progress other than by burning the tree. City and state officials in affected areas have declared all-out war on the beetles, determined to keep them from spreading.

Many of the long-horned beetles grow quite large, even without counting the antennae that can double or triple their overall length. One, the South American giant long-horned beetle—its scientific name, *Titanus giganteus*, gives even those who do not know Latin a clue to its most distinguishing characteristic—is the longest beetle and among the longest insects in the world. It can reportedly stretch nearly 8 inches (20 cm), end to end.

Leaf Beetles (family Chrysomelidae)

By some counts, this is the second-largest beetle family. By other counts, it falls into third or fourth place. But there is no question that it contains a huge number of beetle species, all of them leaf eaters, and many of them a serious problem for gardeners and farmers.

The common names for this family's members often reflect their leafy food preferences. For example, there is the bean leaf beetle, the cottonwood leaf beetle, the elm leaf beetle, and so on. Other names reveal the threatened crop: the Colorado potato beetle, the asparagus beetle, the cucumber beetle—the list goes on and on. It is hard to find a garden plant that some member of this family does not attack. Their favorite foods include corn, squash, eggplant, cabbage, broccoli, spinach, cauliflower, and radish.

Obviously, these beetles are not among most people's favorite insects. But they do have some endearing traits. One is that, among beetles, they are probably the best at playing dead.

As soon as a leaf beetle is threatened, it drops to the ground and becomes the perfect picture of an ex-beetle.

One leaf eater, the golden tortoise beetle, goes a step further. It not only plays dead, it also changes its color like a chameleon. From its normal shiny gold, it turns a muted violet or brown. Several of its relatives have similar color-changing skills.

Weevils (family Curculionidae)

With a roll call of more than 50,000 species, the weevils win the prize for being the beetles' biggest bunch. To be precise, Curculionidae is the largest family in the largest order (Coleoptera) in the largest class (Insecta) in the entire kingdom of Animalia. The weevils make up the largest family of animals on Earth.

Their numbers alone hint at their incredible variety. Their dominant presence also hints at the reasons for the beetles' success: an ability to adapt their size, shape, and behavior to take advantage of any available food source and habitat.

Weevils are not always easy to see—many are quite small— but when viewed closely, the shape of their head is distinctive. It is extended into a long snout, with the chewing mouthparts at the tip. Usually, the antennae are out near the tip also. The long, slender snout is designed for an insect that specializes in boring into stems, leaves, roots, fruits, and seeds.

Some weevils are so stretched out as to seem distinctly weird. The oddest is probably the New Zealand beetle known as the giraffe weevil, a name that easily suggests the shape of this weevil's front end.

Most people are more concerned with the weevils' diet than their looks. From the human point of view, this family contains many destructive, and thus expensive, insects. Weevils damage or destroy a huge variety of food crops. Among the most seriously affected are wheat, alfalfa, grapes, blackberries, blueberries, strawberries, apples, pears, peaches, and plums, and that is only an abbreviated list. It does not even include cotton, the favorite food of the boll weevil, one of the most destructive insects in history.

Dung Beetles (family Scarabaeidae)

The most famous members of this family, and the ones who give it their name, are the sacred scarabs, the revered dung beetles of ancient Egypt. Dung beetles are found around the world. They are among Earth's most important recyclers, and they make up the bulk of the family's 30,000 species. Dung beetles are often fairly large, handsomely sleek, colored in an elegant bronze, yellow, or black, and festooned with an array of pointed and forked horns that make them appealing to collectors.

Among the scarabs are some of the world's biggest, heaviest beetles and their names—the elephant beetle, rhinoceros beetle, Hercules beetle, Goliath beetle—reflect their status. Hercules, at 7 inches (18 cm), seems to be the biggest. But Goliath appears to hold the record for being the heaviest. Although it measures a mere 5 inches (13 cm), it reportedly has weighed in at a whopping 3.5 ounces (100 g)—nearly a quarter pound.

Dung is a food source that is never in short supply, and it has served the scarabs well. But with beetles as with people, there is no accounting for taste. Some scarabs are part-time scavengers. A few are predators. Tropical giants such as Goliath and Hercules and their kin apparently grow big on tree sap. At some point in their evolution, other members of the family switched over to a plant diet also. Among them are a couple of beetles quite familiar to American gardeners.

THE RHINOCEROS BEETLE, LIKE OTHER LARGE DUNG BEETLES, EATS PLANTS. IT IS ALSO THE STRONGEST BEETLE, ABLE TO PULL AT LEAST ONE HUNDRED TIMES ITS OWN WEIGHT.

The first is generally known as the June bug, though some people call it the May beetle. The different names come from the beetle's customary appearance in either month, depending on local temperatures. Most people also call the June bug a general nuisance (or something worse), since it eats a lot of different leaves and is hard to catch in the act. June bugs start their destructive activity as grubs buried in the soil. They stay there for up to four years, eating the roots of nearly anything that grows. Even when they finally emerge as adults, they bury themselves again during the day and come out only at night.

Another well-known non-dung-eating scarab is a relative newcomer to the United States. The Japanese beetle first appeared on—actually, *in*—American soil in 1916, in the city of Riverton, New Jersey. It probably arrived as a stowaway in a shipment of plants imported from Japan. Because this large copper-colored beetle is a voracious eater of plants, state officials tried to keep it from spreading. They drew a border around an oval-shaped zone one-half to one mile (.8 to 1.6 km) from where the beetle was initially found. Then they burned or sprayed with insecticide every plant within the zone. Following that, they kept careful watch. Over the next few years, they caught and killed millions of the beetles, farther and farther from the original target area. Finally, in 1920, they gave up.

Today, Japanese beetles are an inevitable presence in nearly every garden, farm, and park in every state east of the Mississippi. They have also appeared in spots throughout the Midwest, as well as in Oregon and California. These beetles are not terribly picky eaters—they dine on more than 300 different kinds of plants, and they are equally satisfied with any part of the plant, from flowers to stems to leaves to fruits. The Japanese beetle menu includes maple, oak, and sycamore trees; apple, cherry, and peach trees; roses, zinnias, and marigolds; raspberries, grapes, and cantaloupes; corn, clover, soybeans, and much, much more.

One might think that Japan, where the beetle lived for eons before extending its range to the United States, would hardly have a green leaf left. But in Japan the beetle is not much of a problem, since there it has a small army of natural predators that keep it under control. Unfortunately, none of the Japanese flies and wasps that feed on the beetle seem to do very well in the United States. Insects imported from other Asian countries have shown some promise, though, and in recent years gardeners have had success with a species of beetle-killing bacteria discovered, fittingly, in New Jersey.

A JUNE BUG IS ONE SCARAB THAT HUMANS GENERALLY DISLIKE, SINCE IT IS A VORACIOUS EATER OF MANY PLANTS AND FLOWERS.

Rove Beetles (family Staphylinidae)

The family of rove beetles is quite large—more than 26,000 species—but it avoids the limelight. Rove beetles are mostly nocturnal creatures that prefer moist, dark places. They also like to hang around decaying fruit, decaying animal bodies, and dung, habits that tend to keep them away from our notice. Still, anyone who has seen quickly scurrying creatures exposed in a kicked-over leaf pile has no doubt encountered them. Many people see dull-colored rove beetles and mistake them for something else—often insects called earwigs—because they are not very beetle-like in appearance. Although a few grow as big as 1.5 inches (4 cm), most are in the quarter-inch (7-mm) range. They are generally flat and slender, have short wing covers, and a fairly flexible abdomen, which they often flex upward when threatened, as if they had a stinger at the tip. (They do not; the defensive response is a bluff.)

Despite their association with rotting food, carrion, and dung, most rove beetles are actually predators. What they are after are the fly larvae, or maggots, that hatch from eggs laid in these food sources, and they hunt them down relentlessly. Members of one interesting group of beetles within the family do not hunt down their prey as much as persuade their prey to take them home. These are rove beetles that specialize in making friends with ants.

Ants are not easy food. Worker ants are aggressive, they have stingers, and their bodies are filled with toxic acid. But ants are also governed by pheromones, chemical substances that identify members of the ant colony to one another and tell them how to behave.

The ant-loving rove beetles produce two pheromones that mimic the ants' signals. The first pheromone, when picked up by any ant that rushes out to attack the invading beetle, tells the ant to calm down, immediately. The second pheromone is identical to one produced by ant larvae. In effect, it tells the now calm ant that the beetle is actually a baby ant and that it needs to be taken care of.

The ant, like the good social worker it is, quickly obliges. It picks up the beetle and carries it to the ant nursery, where the beetle lets itself be cared for. Eventually, the beetle is left alone to do whatever it wants—which is to start consuming real ant larvae and eggs.

The rove beetles have a good life in the ant nest. They lay their eggs there, and when they hatch, the beetle grubs produce

ROVE BEETLES OFTEN DO NOT LOOK LIKE BEETLES. THIS *STENUS* HAS BULGING EYES, SHORT ELYTRA, AND A LONG ABDOMEN, MAKING IT RESEMBLE AN ANT OR EARWIG— ITS PREY.

the same pheromones as the adults do, so the ants take care of the young beetles too.

Darkling Beetles (family Tenebrionidae)

Unlike the rove beetles, darkling beetles usually like dry spots. Many of the species in this large family actually like very dry spots—they are desert dwellers. To survive in such environments, they have developed several typical features. They often

A DARKLING BEETLE FROM IRAN DISPLAYS A COMMON FEATURE OF THE FAMILY: A
THICK, HEAVILY ARMORED EXOSKELETON TO CONSERVE MOISTURE AND TO PROTECT IT.

have unusually long legs, so that they can get their bodies as far
as possible above the hot sand. Protecting them from their harsh
surroundings is a skin—made of the outer layers of their
exoskeleton—that is extremely tough, even for a beetle.

The ironclad beetle, which lives in the deserts of the
American Southwest, is one of this group. Its skin is so thick that
it reminded people of the Civil War ships that were plated with
iron to make them invulnerable to enemy cannon fire.

Desert beetles often bury themselves in the sand during the
heat of the day, and their skin takes a lot of abuse from rubbing
against the coarse sand particles. Their skin is also usually coat-
ed with a kind of wax, to keep them waterproof. The purpose is
not to keep water out, but to keep it in, so that they do not dry
out and die.

Not all darkling beetles live in the desert. Many live much closer to our homes. A great many live *in* our homes, to be exact, in the sheltered, dry environments of our kitchen cabinets.

Flour beetles, like their desert-dwelling cousins, do not need to search for water to drink. They absorb whatever they require from the air. Flour beetles could just as easily be called pasta beetles, cracker beetles, or chocolate beetles. They could be named after dried fruit or dried peas, for that matter. They can live off all those items and much else that they find in a typical pantry. These particular darkling beetles have become so accustomed to living off our stored foods—they have been found in food stored in a pharaoh's 4,500-year-old tomb—that it is hard to imagine how they ever got along without us.

Flour beetles are small. The largest one is only four-tenths of an inch (10 mm), and the smallest is a quarter that size. But they make up in numbers what they lack in size. They can go from egg to adult in about five weeks, and a single female can lay a thousand eggs during her three-year life span. Since they may not face a host of predators in the wilds of a typical kitchen cabinet, a healthy number of those eggs can hatch, grow, lay eggs of their own, and take over yet another bag of something delectable in the cabinet. In this particular battle with beetles over food, it is probably best to just let the beetles keep it—but somewhere away from the house.

On the other hand, there are occasions for bringing a bunch of darkling beetles into the house, and many people do so regularly. The larvae of darkling beetles are commonly called mealworms, and though they are not worms at all, they are certainly meals for millions of housebound pet fish and turtles.

6 Meet More Beetles

J ust because two-thirds of all beetle species belong to a mere eight large families, that hardly means the other 150 or so families are filled with rare beasties. Among the "smaller" beetle families is that of the familiar ladybugs (Coccinellidae)—it holds about 5,000 different round-bodied relatives, which means there are more different ladybugs than there are mammals. Then there is the tiny family of fireflies (Lampyridae). It has a scant 2,000 members.

To describe all the families would take a very, very large book. A description of nine more families, however, will at least help to portray the diversity of beetle life.

Wood-boring Beetles (family Anobiidae)

Most of the beetles in this family are no bigger than .33 inch (8 mm) long, colored a not very noticeable black or brown, and spend their whole lives boring into pieces of wood. The death-watch beetles belong to this family. These are the beetles that

IN SOUTHEAST ASIA, A FIREFLY TREE PRESENTS THE SPECTACULAR SIGHT OF THOUSANDS OF FIREFLIES BLINKING IN UNISON; THE DISPLAY CAN GO ON EVERY NIGHT FOR MONTHS.

beat their heads against the walls of their tunnels, advertising for mates. Among their kin are the furniture beetles, and though they usually lead quiet lives, they can sometimes make a dramatic, noisy appearance.

Unlike some wood-chewing insects, furniture beetles do not much care whether the wood they inhabit is part of a living tree or dead, cut-up lumber. They simply bore into any board available. Within the tunnels, female furniture beetles lay their eggs. After hatching, the larvae carve out their own tiny tunnels inside the wood, until they grow up and produce a new generation of borers. This can go on for years, without any outward signs of all this activity. In the meantime, the wood can be turned into a bookcase, a cabinet, a rocking horse, or a beam in a house. The human owners of the beetles' home, unfortunately, rarely become aware of their unwanted tenants until the beetles' home, and sometimes the humans' home, starts falling apart.

Two other members of the family deserve mention, not because they will eat anyone's home but because they will eat practically anything in it. The drugstore beetle, like the flour beetle of the darkling family, loves the contents of kitchen cabinets (as well as, presumably, drugstores). It too will gorge itself on anything dry, from soup mixes to nuts. It loves cereal, bread crumbs, spaghetti, rice, and spices—it will not sneeze at an offering of pepper or turn down a helping of the hottest chili powder.

The drugstore beetle's relative, the tobacco beetle, goes a step further. Although it is content with its cousin's diet, it is happiest when it has some dried tobacco to chew on. Cigars or cigarettes are pure bliss to this beetle, despite tobacco's generally being as bad for insects as it is for people. A liquid solution of nicotine—a key tobacco ingredient—has long been used by people as an insecticide.

Ladybugs (family Coccinellidae)

The ladybugs—or ladybirds, as they are called in Great Britain—are among everyone's favorite beetles, all over the world. Gardeners and farmers especially love them, thanks to their bottomless appetite for aphids and other plant-killing insects. Ladybugs also gobble up the eggs of some major crop killers, including the Colorado potato beetle and the alfalfa weevil.

The roughly 5,000 ladybug species are so adored by so many people that it hardly seems fair to point out that there are a couple of members of the family that are not nearly as considerate of human needs as they might be.

The chief culprit is the Mexican bean beetle. Although it looks deceptively like its red, rounded, black-spotted, bug-eating cousins, this particular ladybug is a vegetarian, and it would much rather eat a bean plant than any aphids it finds on it. Despite its name, the Mexican bean beetle is not confined to Mexico. It has spread all over North America and become a serious problem for soybean growers.

Carpet Beetles (family Dermestidae)

This family is made up of dedicated recyclers, so one might think its members would be as beloved as ladybugs. But most people regard them with different emotions.

As their name indicates, a number of species in the family like to inhabit a warm, wooly world, especially when it is cold outside. In a rug, they are as snug as a beetle can be. But they will also make their homes inside stuffed furniture or warm clothing. Unfortunately, they like to eat their homes. Knowing that the beetles are just doing what they must does not calm

TINY HAIRS ON A CARPET BEETLE LARVA ARE IRRITATING TO PREDATORS AND PEOPLE ALIKE—MANY HUMANS HAVE ALLERGIC REACTIONS TO THEM.

people who see their expensive carpets, couches, and cardigans reduced to dust.

Carpet beetles are scavengers, making use of what other animals leave behind. They dine on fur, hair, feathers, dried flakes of skin, and the bodies of dead insects and larger animals. Outside, their dining habits make them delightful custodians in a messy natural world. They are among Earth's most important recycling organisms, breaking down animals' remains and returning the nutrients to the soil. Inside, however, those same habits make them most unwelcome.

Yet there are places where these beetles are invited guests. All over the world, natural history museums find the beetles' fondness for dead flesh invaluable. Curators use the beetles to clean every bit of material from animal bones before they put the bones on display. Museum workers have to keep the beetles on a tight leash, though. Any beetles that wander away from the bone-cleaning rooms often find a feast of feather- or fur-filled display cases nearby.

Diving Beetles (family Dysticidae)

More than most other insect orders, the beetles feature species that have evolved to live in ponds, lakes, streams, and rivers. This family is one of several made up completely of water-dwelling beetles.

Perhaps their most noteworthy feature is the one that allows them to breathe. Underneath their hard elytra, diving beetles have a hollowed-out space that they use for holding a bubble of air. Whenever a diver needs a refill, it swims to the surface and pokes its abdomen above the water. Air flows into the hollow space and is trapped by the wing covers. The beetle can then go back underwater and continue its business. For the divers, "business" means hunting.

Like other water-based beetles, the predatory divers have flat, sleek bodies designed for slicing through the water. They also have flattened, feathered rear legs, which they use as oars to power themselves. Those oars make them strong swimmers, and diving beetles can chase down not only other insects but also tadpoles, small fish, and shrimp. Once they catch up with their prey, their powerful jaws make short work of the meal.

Whirligigs (family Gyrinidae)

Other water-dwelling beetle families differ from the predatory divers in many ways, including how they hoard their air supply. Some trap air with their legs, holding a bubble under their abdomen; others employ a covering of fine hairs to trap a

bubble of air around their entire body. The whirligigs do away with the problem completely by simply staying on the surface.

Whirligigs are virtually unsinkable, thanks to a water-repellent coating on their upper body. This coating allows them to float naturally, half in and half out of the water, simultaneously on the lookout for danger and food. They can do both at the same time because whirligigs are graced with highly unusual eyes. Each is divided in two, top and bottom, so that the whirligig essentially has four eyes instead of two. The top eyes are focused to see through air; the bottom two are adjusted to see through water.

Like the diving beetles, the whirligigs are predators, but they have an odd method of hunting. They stay on the surface, swimming in circles. (They *can* swim underwater, and do occasionally, but they have to work hard to keep from bouncing back up.) Their seemingly dull-witted strategy makes them look like far less skillful hunters than the powerful diving beetles. Yet the whirligigs' technique is more sophisticated than one might suppose. While swimming with their middle and rear legs, whirligigs kick up rows of tiny waves that spread outward in a circle. With their upper eyes, the beetles keep a watch for anything that interferes with the regular pattern of the little waves. Anything that does interfere the beetles assume is food, and they quickly swim over to investigate. They are helped in this hunt by their antennae, which are sensitive to the faintest vibrations.

Click Beetles (family Elateridae)

The click beetles have a dual reputation. As long, skinny, hard-skinned larvae, they gnaw at the roots of many crops, including beans, corn, and potatoes, and they are intensely disliked by farmers and gardeners. Making matters worse is that these larvae are slow to mature; they can hang around in the soil for as long as eight years. Collectively, these destructive insects are known as wireworms, a name that sounds as tough and as unpleasant as they are. As adults, however, click beetles do not eat much at all, and many people find them not only tolerable but entertaining.

Their appeal lies in their escape tactics. When adult click beetles land on their back, as they seem to do rather often when falling to the ground to escape a predator, they turn themselves over by a very strange, and unique, mechanism. They arch their back so that their flexible thorax sticks up into the air. Then they slap their body back down on the ground, as fast and as hard as they can. The object of their exercise is to force a hooked spine on the "belly" side of their thorax into a specially shaped groove. The spine does not slide into the groove easily or smoothly. Just

PRESUMABLY, THE TWO LARGE "EYESPOTS" ON THIS EASTERN EYED CLICK BEETLE
STARTLE A PREDATOR AND GIVE THE BEETLE TIME TO GET AWAY.

the opposite—it meets a lot of resistance, until enough pressure
builds up and it suddenly snaps in with a "click" loud enough to
be heard. The force of the sudden snap flips the beetle end over
end into the air. With luck, when it lands, it will be right side up.

Unfortunately, click beetles end up on their back again as
often as they land on their feet. But a wrong-side-up click beetle
will simply perform its self-righting maneuver again and again,

until it finally lands right side up and can walk away. Presumably, this behavior is as confusing to predators as to human observers.

All species of click beetles are slender and straight-sided. Usually they are dull colored and small—less than an inch (2.5 cm) long—but a few species are bigger and brighter. A handful are very bright—they are known as headlight beetles, and they produce light from two organs on either side of the prothorax.

Fireflies (family Lampyridae)

Along with ladybugs, fireflies are probably the favorite beetles of children, who are fascinated by the insects' blinking lights. The wonderful lights range in color from green to yellow to almost red, depending on the species. Most fireflies have a single light located at the tip of their slender abdomen. But some of the family's 2,000 species have more. One has twenty-two greenish lights dotting its thorax and abdomen and a pair of red lights on its head to cap off the display.

A firefly's flashes are a form of insect instant messaging between appropriate males and females. Each species has its own distinctive light color and code—different species flash on and off in different sequences and rhythms—allowing males and females of the same species to find each other in the darkness of night.

But females of several firefly species have manipulated the system for purposes other than mating. They have learned to imitate the blinking pattern of a different species and thus to lure unsuspecting males to their side. These female fireflies are predators. They sit patiently on bushes or stalks of high grass, blinking out their phony identity code. Males responding to the imposters' signals fly over and land. What they find is a hungry beetle in search of a meal, not a mate.

Stag Beetles (family Lucanidae)

The stag beetles are among the true showstoppers in the long parade of beetle families. Many are of considerable size—more than two inches (5 cm) long—and are elegantly decked out in glossy black, two-toned black and yellow, or shining bronze. But it is their huge, menacing mandibles that demand attention and give the group its name. These oversized jaws were thought to resemble the elaborate antlers of male deer, or stags.

Even though the six-legged stags' headgear are mouthparts and not antlers, their name is still appropriate. Despite their

ALL STAG BEETLES ARE CHARACTERIZED BY OVERSIZED MANDIBLES, BUT ONLY THE MALES GROW JAWS THIS LARGE.

menacing look, stag beetles, like deer, are plant eaters. (Actually, their chief food is dead wood, and they are among the important beetle members of the forest recycling team.) Also, like deer, male stag beetles use their headgear to battle other males in their quest for mates. That is not to say that the beetle's jaws cannot deliver a meaningful bite. When threatened, stag beetles raise their heads and open their jaws defiantly. A predator, or a person, who assumes that this display is a bluff would be making a mistake.

Among stag beetles, the males are the ones with the biggest jaws, just as male deer are the ones that grow the impressive rack of antlers. But size does not always matter. Though the female stag beetles have smaller mandibles than the males do, they deliver the more powerful, more painful bite.

Carrion Beetles (family Silphidae)

The species that make up this family, along with their flesh-eating cousins, the carpet beetles, are among the world's great recyclers of life's nutrients. Carrion—the flesh of dead animals— is not a pleasant thing to think about, and the animals that survive on it seldom enjoy good reputations among us. Vultures, for instance, are rarely the heroes in children's stories. Yet, if the Earth is not to be covered with mountains of rotting meat, something must dispose of the legions of animals that die every hour. In the natural world, that job is chiefly performed by fungi, bacteria, and insects, with the carrion-eating beetles playing a major role.

Carrion beetles form a small family of fewer than 250 species. Among these, the most notable is the select group known as the burying beetles, with their very complex parenting behavior. They not only feed on carrion, they take great pains to bury it to keep it away from other interested diners. They also

THE CARRION-EATING AMERICAN BURYING BEETLE HAS BECOME AN ENDANGERED SPECIES AS ITS NATURAL FOREST HABITAT HAS SHRUNK ACROSS MUCH OF THE COUNTRY.

often work in pairs, and they work not just for themselves but for the benefit of their future offspring.

Males are generally the food finders, and they operate at night. They have a remarkable sensitivity to odors and can find a body quickly, within an hour of the animal's death, from a distance of about two miles (3.3 km). Usually more than one male beetle arrives at the scene. Once there, they release pheromones that signal female beetles in the area to join them. Then all the beetles start competing to see who gets the prized meat. The biggest male and female are most often the winners, and they start working as a team to bury the body and prepare a nest for their young.

Their first task is to determine how hard the ground is below the body. If it is soft enough, the beetles start excavating a hole directly beneath the dead animal. If it is too hard, the beetles move the body to a more suitable spot by getting beneath it, turning onto their backs, and using their legs to inch the load along. These beetles are not big—the biggest is about 1.4 inches (35 mm), and most are between .4 and one inch (10 to 25 mm). Despite their small size, though, they are very strong. A burying beetle is able to move an animal weighing 3.5 to 7 ounces (100 to 200 g), which translates into a bird the size of a quail or a robin.

Before burial, the beetles prepare the body by removing fur or feathers, feet or wings, and skin. They then shape the remaining flesh into a ball, coat it with a fluid that keeps it from decaying quickly, and dig out a chamber large enough to hold it. Within a day or two after burial, the female lays her eggs in a small chamber she digs above the ball. Over the following three to four days, both the male and the female feed on the meat and then regurgitate, or vomit, drops of the partially digested food into a cavity they have hollowed out on the top of the ball. The drops form a pool of liquid that will feed the larvae.

Burying beetles tend their young much as birds do their chicks. When the grubs hatch, the adults feed them and guard over them for a week or so, until the young beetles are ready to enter their pupal stage. At that point the grubs crawl off to bury themselves nearby, and the parents dig their way out of the nest and back to the surface, ready to begin the whole cycle of death and life all over again.

7 Beetles and Us

Ⓞne of the reasons beetles have been so successful as a group is that they have proved to be enormously adaptable. More than any other group of animals, they have evolved to take advantage of any major change in the planet's landscape. When, 145 million years ago, flowering plants began to spread over the land, beetles appeared that could thrive not just on the flowers but on nearly every part of every plant. When reptiles and, later, mammals appeared, beetles evolved forms that could feed on them directly, on the food they left behind, or on their wastes. When humans appeared and eventually started planting crops, domesticating animals, and building storehouses and homes, beetles found ways to exploit these resources as well.

Today, despite all our knowledge and sophistication, beetles are among our most powerful competitors for food. Insects in general end up eating as much as one half of all the food we grow. Although we do not know precisely how much of that damage is caused specifically by beetles, the amount is obviously enormous. Beetles of various species devour our wheat, barley, oats, corn, rice, alfalfa, potatoes, tomatoes, cucumbers, melons,

BEETLES AND HUMANS HAVE DEPENDED ON ONE ANOTHER AND BATTLED
ONE ANOTHER SINCE THE VERY BEGINNINGS OF CIVILIZATION.

squash, beans, peas, apples, plums, figs, cherries, and grapes—there is nothing we plant for food that beetles too do not find desirable. In addition, they attack crops planted not for food but for textiles and clothing.

A prime example of destructive beetle power is the boll weevil, one of the most devastating insects ever to invade the United States. The boll weevil was not a native of this country originally. In the early 1800s it was found no farther north than Veracruz, Mexico. But throughout the nineteenth century, as Americans planted more and more cotton across the South, the boll weevil gradually came closer. It took the beetle more than sixty years, but by 1892 it had crossed the Rio Grande into Brownsville, Texas. Within another thirty years it was laying waste to cotton fields all across the southeastern United States. Since the 1920s it has continued to spread, west to California, and south and east to Venezuela, Colombia, and Brazil.

The boll weevil is so destructive because it feeds on more than one part of the cotton plant and at more than one stage in its growth. In the spring, female weevils start chewing holes into the young cotton buds, where they lay their eggs. When the eggs hatch, the emerging larvae hungrily eat though the buds they find themselves in. Within three weeks, they become adults; then they spread out to devour more buds. Later, after the plants have grown, the beetles attack the bolls—the seed pods—and in these the female weevils lay still more eggs. Weevils reproduce quickly: ten generations may be born in a single cotton growing season.

A boll weevil is a small beetle, a mere .25 inch (6 mm) long. But its impact is huge. It costs cotton growers hundreds of millions of dollars each year, counting the costs both of the lost cotton and of the insecticides bought to stop the destruction. People have attempted to defeat the boll weevil in many ways over the years. Their efforts have ranged from all-out chemical warfare to bringing in ants and wasps they thought might feed on weevil larvae or eggs. But nothing has been more than partly successful. Despite all our human cleverness, the tiny boll weevil continues to fight us to a standstill.

The boll weevil is one of the more spectacular examples of a beetle pest, but it is far from the only one. Everything we grow draws its own mob of beetles to war against. Destructive as these insects are, however, they represent only one side of our relationship with beetles. In truth, people have traditionally found beetles to be much more helpful than harmful.

Beetles as Food

Beetles may eat many of our plants, but we in turn eat a lot of beetles. Though few people in the United States grab a handful of beetles when in search of a snack, people in other parts of the world have long considered beetles and, especially, beetle larvae delicacies. Throughout Asia and Africa, in Australia, New Guinea, and the islands of the South Pacific, across Central and South America, people continue to make good use of this abundant food source. Beetle dishes have largely disappeared north of Mexico, but at one time beetles were part of the standard diet of Native Americans. Their favorite recipe called for the larvae of certain long-horned beetles. It was, and is, a healthy choice. Like all insects, beetles are high in protein and low in fat—and the larvae are a lot less crunchy than the adults.

Recipes for beetle larvae appear in cultures around the globe. They call for grubs to be breaded, toasted, roasted, rolled into sausages, boiled into soup, mixed with rice, or just eaten raw. Even the ancient Romans liked to rustle up some grubs. They were so fond of them that they took the time to fatten

up the grubs before cooking them by feeding them flour mixed with wine. Apparently, the cooked grubs tasted something like almonds.

In Sickness and in Health

Beetles have often gone down human throats as medicine as well as food. Until modern times, it was not at all unusual to believe that beetles could help cure a wide range of diseases, from measles and malaria to ear- and toothaches. Some supposed cures required the patient to wear a symbolically powerful beetle—often a scarab—or at least its literally power-ful jaws, over a specific part of the body. Other remedies called for grinding up beetles into mixtures that were to be drunk or eaten.

All such cures were based on superstition. Although there are indeed many good uses for beetles, there is no scientific reason for thinking that treating illness is one of them. Still, swal-lowing a beetle or two probably did few people any harm, even if it did not do them any real good.

The one exception is the use of blister beetles, which pro-duce the burning substance cantharidin. There may actually be some benefit to weak cantharidin-based ointments used to treat some skin conditions. But in strong enough doses, the substance quickly reveals how blister beetles got their name, and it can be very toxic if swallowed. Probably precisely because mixtures made from blister beetles can be so painful, they were recom-mended as treatment for ailments as serious as epilepsy, rabies, and asthma. (The mistaken logic was "If it hurts, or tastes bad, it must be good for you.")

Beetles in Fashion

One of the attractions of beetles is the spectacular colors many of them sport. In pursuit of adornments for their clothing and jewelry, people have eagerly chased after beetles through the ages. The shining, brilliantly colored wing covers of the jewel beetles, in particular, have been enormously popular among the fashion-conscious. Native peoples of Central and South America string the elytra into earrings, necklaces, and hair orna-ments. In India, Sri Lanka, Thailand, and other Southeast Asian countries, the red, green, blue, bronze, and silver elytra have been sewn into delicate fabrics that are worn on festive occasions.

In the nineteenth century, beetle adornment became a fad in England. A craze for collecting beetle specimens already existed among educated British men. During the early and mid 1800s, the study of the natural world in general was a popular occupation of British gentlemen. Charles Darwin himself—the "father" of evolution—was a fanatic beetle collector as a young man. His passion for beetles actually drew him to the serious study of nature in the first place. This was also the time when the British empire extended into India and Asia, and magnificent

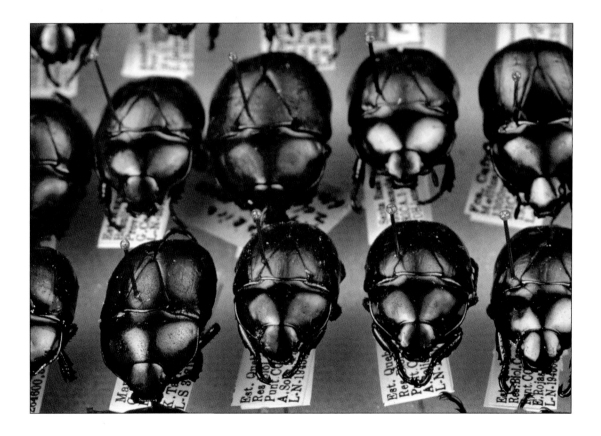

COLORFUL SCARABS SUCH AS THESE CENTRAL AMERICAN CHRISTMAS BEETLES CAN BE RAISED ON FARMS TO MEET THE DEMAND OF COLLECTORS.

beetle fabrics and jewelry were introduced to the most fashionable women in London. Trendsetters of the time had shining beetle jewelry and shawls designed for them. Some even took up the new fashion of wearing live colorful beetles attached to a pin or clip by a thin gold chain.

Wearing live jewels was new only in Europe. In other parts of the world, people had come up with the idea of living decorations long before. In Mexico and Central America, people followed the age-old fashion of gluing brightly colored beads onto a beetle, then putting the beetle on a thin chain leash that was pinned to their clothing.

They also employed glowing fireflies and click beetles for jewelry, as did people throughout South America and the islands of the West Indies. They would attach these living lights to pins or gather them in gauze bags, which they would then attach to their clothing or wear in their hair.

Finally there were, and are, people who keep live beetles not as precious jewels but as pampered pets. Japanese children have traditionally kept and cared for favored beetles, particularly the larger horned species such as stag beetles and rhinoceros beetles. In recent years, pet-beetle boasting has become trendy among adults as well. Popular beetles, such as a six-inch-long (15-cm) Hercules beetle, may cost more than $100. Bigger or especially rare beetles may cost hundreds or even thousands of dollars more.

High-Tech Beetles

More serious-minded humans also collect beetles. For scientists teasing out the secrets of DNA, the genes that control the fireflies flashing lights have become a standard tool. By attaching the genes to others in organisms ranging from plants to mice, researchers can literally see when and how genes are signaled to turn on and off.

Likewise, researchers developing new high-tech materials have been studying the fascinating survival skills of the stenocara beetle. This member of the darkling beetle family lives in the harsh, dry Namib Desert of Africa, a place where water is nearly impossible to find. Yet the beetle never suffers from thirst. It simply makes its own water, from the fog that rolls over the desert in the early morning.

The beetle's back, the scientists discovered, is covered with tiny bumps made of two different substances—one that attracts water and one that repels it. Together the bumps gather moisture from the fog and collect it in tiny drops. The beetle, which walks with its rear end tilted higher than its front end, simply lets the drops roll down its back and into its mouth. The scientists hope that the beetle's methods could one day turn out to be helpful to people. If we could make large nets, for instance, out of a material similar to the covering on the beetle's back, then perhaps people living in arid areas could inexpensively produce water from fog also.

Working for Humans

The most important human use of beetles, though, is as a natural form of pest control. Farmers around the world have known of beneficial insect-eating beetles since ancient times, and they learned how to encourage local beetle predators to come feast on the insects devouring their crops. The first instance of someone deliberately importing a beetle from one part of the world to use in another seems to have been in the late 1880s. At the time, an insect called the cottony cushion scale was destroying groves of orange and lemon trees in California. Scale insects are

USING BEETLES TO BATTLE OTHER INSECTS HARMFUL TO CROPS REDUCES THE NEED FOR CHEMICAL PESTICIDES. THIS LADYBUG PREYS ON POTATO BEETLE EGGS.

relatives of aphids, and this particular scale had accidentally arrived in California along with a shipment of acacia trees. Because no native scale predator existed in California, the insects kept eating and multiplying. The brilliant solution was to bring over predators from the scale's home. Originally, just 129 ladybugs were let loose on a farm outside Los Angeles as an experiment. The results were so promising that within months thousands more ladybugs were released throughout the state, and California's orange and lemon trees were saved.

Over the past century, people have employed many more beetle species for pest control. The beetles' job is not always to eat insects—sometimes they are used to rid farms and gardens of unwanted weeds. Beetles have evolved to eat nearly everything edible on Earth. Somewhere, no matter what the nature of the unwanted invader, there is probably a beetle ready to dine on it.

The vastly underrated dung beetle has made that point repeatedly. These waste eaters come in many varieties. Some are generalists, happy to eat the dung of many different animals. Some are specialists, fastidious beetles that will consider only the especially tasty waste of a specific animal. One South American dung beetle, for instance, is so dedicated to the wastes of the three-toed tree sloth that it lives near the source of its food, in the sloth's fur.

By the middle of the twentieth century, Australia was a land that, while rich in ladybugs, was poor in dung beetles—at least, dung beetles that found the wastes of cows delightful. There were plenty of beetles hungry for the dung of kangaroos and other native animals. But apparently there were none with a taste for the plentiful offerings of the cattle that British settlers had started bringing to Australia back in the 1780s. For many years, the herds were small enough that the tendency of those cows' wastes to just stick around was only a minor annoyance. But by the 1960s Australia was home to many millions of cows, and it was being plastered hourly by an appropriate number of cow patties.

This created a serious problem. The dung took years to break down naturally, and it prevented new growth of the grass the cows needed to graze on. (Until something breaks down the wastes into smaller pieces, and works it into the soil, it is useless as fertilizer.) Even more seriously, the abundance of dung resulted in an abundance of disease-carrying flies, which found the cow patties perfect sites for their eggs.

To combat the problem, the Australian government started a worldwide search for dung eaters that would thrive in Australia's dry climate. Eventually scientists found them among the dung beetles of South Africa. They also found beetles that would eat the fly larvae that hatched from the eggs laid in the cattle dung.

Beetles are hugely important in keeping our world free of not only excess waste but of dead bodies as well. Most of us have probably given little thought to what happens to all the animals that die on Earth every day. We assume that they are all somehow "naturally recycled," and this is indeed true. But among the chief recyclers are many species of beetles, including the burying beetles. They and other carrion eaters quickly find and use materials we might prefer not to deal with.

Beetles for Tomorrow

With hundreds of thousands of beetle species and uncountable trillions of individual beetles, the beetles' future should seem assured. Yet the sad fact is that some beetles, like so many other animals, are threatened by people's increasing use of the planet. In the United States alone, as of 2007, the federal government listed seventeen beetle species as threatened or endangered; and it was considering adding another fifteen species to the list. Among the most critically endangered is the American burying

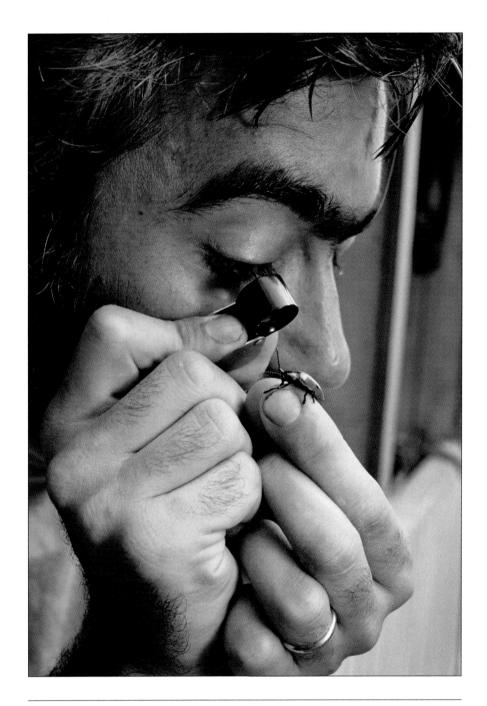

EVERY YEAR, SCIENTISTS DISCOVER THOUSANDS OF NEW BEETLE SPECIES. THIS PREVI-
OUSLY UNKNOWN BEETLE WAS FOUND IN A NATURE PRESERVE IN PERU.

beetle, an inch-long (25-mm) orange-splotched black beetle that once called thirty-seven states, including the entire northeast quarter of the country, its home. But as much of its natural habitat has disappeared, so have the beetles. Today they are found only in isolated spots.

Worldwide, there is no telling how many beetle species are threatened—or how many have already disappeared. Some of the danger comes from collectors who are eager for rare species. The South African Cape stag beetle is one of those. Determined collectors have paid as much as thousands of dollars for this shiny, all-black beetle with its huge, odd-shaped jaws and plus-size front legs.

But the loss of its natural habitat is the chief cause of any beetle's troubles. This is an increasingly urgent problem everywhere as human populations continue to grow. Nowhere is it more serious, though, than in those areas where the tropical rain forests are disappearing. These are habitats that are duplicated nowhere else on Earth. They are also those areas where the diversity of beetle species is greatest.

No doubt, as a group, beetles will continue to thrive on the planet until the end of its days, no matter what we humans may do to them. But we should keep in mind that we are rather new arrivals on Earth. As a species, we humans arrived in a world already finely crafted by many millions of years of beetle evolution. It is only fitting that while we are here we show them some respect—and perhaps some gratitude.

Glossary

arthropod—a member of the Arthropoda, the largest phylum of animals on Earth, all of which have jointed legs and a body divided into segments; insects form the biggest class of arthropods

bioluminescence—the ability of a living thing, such as a firefly, to produce light

carrion—the flesh of a dead animal

chitin—the hard material that forms an insect's exoskeleton

coevolution—a form of evolution in which changes in one group, such as plants, force changes in another group, such as insects

Coleoptera—the large category, or order, of insects that includes all the beetles

crop—a section of the digestive tube where food is first partially digested and sometimes stored

elytra—the hardened front wings that serve as a shield for the flying wings of a beetle

exoskeleton—the tough outer covering of an arthropod, which protects and provides support for the body

frass—waste products expelled by beetles

ganglion (plural, ganglia)—a cluster of nerve cells

gizzard—muscular section of the digestive tube where food is ground and crushed

hemolymph—an insect's blood

grub—a beetle larva

labium—the lower lip of an insect's mouth

labrum—the upper lip of an insect's mouth

larva (plural, larvae)—an immature insect, before it becomes an adult

mandibles—the two main jaws of an insect

maxillae—an insect's second pair of jaws

mesothorax—the middle section of the thorax

metamorphosis—a change in body form as the insect reaches maturity

metathorax—the rear section of the thorax

molt—the shedding of the exoskeleton

ocelli—simple eyes, used for detecting light and dark

palps—fingerlike mouthparts used for manipulating and tasting food

paleontologist—a scientist who studies the life of the distant past

pheromone—a chemical signal, similar to an odor, that causes animals to behave in certain ways; male and female insects often use pheromones to attract each other

prothorax—the front section of the thorax

pupa—the final immature stage of an insect that undergoes complete metamorphosis, before it becomes an adult

scarab—a member of the dung beetle family (Scarabidae), or the image of a dung beetle

species—the basic unit of classification that defines a "specific" type of animal or plant

spiracle—an opening in the surface of an insect's body that leads to one of the air tubes, or tracheae

stridulation—production of noise by rubbing body parts, such as elytra, against each other

thorax—the middle of the three sections of the insect's body, to which the legs and wings are attached

trachea (plural, tracheae)—an air-carrying tube inside the insect's body

BEETLE FAMILIES

Order COLEOPTERA

	FAMILY	COMMON NAME
The Ten Largest Beetle Families	**Buprestidae** **Carabidae** **Cerambycidae** **Chrysomelidae** **Coccinelidae** **Curculionidae** **Elateridae** **Scarabaeidae** **Staphylinidae** **Tenebrionidae**	jewel or metallic wood-boring beetles ground and tiger beetles long-horned beetles leaf beetles ladybugs weevils, or snout beetles click beetles dung beetles, scarabs, or chafers rove beetles darkling beetles
Other Particularly Significant Families	**Anobiidae** **Cantharidae** **Dermestidae** **Dytiscidae** **Gyrinidae** **Hydrophilidae** **Lampyridae** **Lucanidae** **Meloidae** **Nitidulidae** **Passalidae** **Phengodidae** **Ptiliidae** **Silphidae**	wood-boring and death-watch beetles soldier beetles carpet and skin beetles predaceous diving beetles whirligigs water scavenger beetles lightning bugs or fireflies stag beetles blister beetles sap beetles bessbugs or bess beetles glowworms feather-winged beetles carrion beetles

	FAMILY	COMMON NAME
Other Representative Families	**Aderidae**	antlike leaf beetles
	Anthicidae	antlike flower beetles
	Attelabidae	leaf-rolling weevils
	Belidae	primitive weevils
	Brentidae	straight-snouted weevils
	Cleridae	checkered beetles
	Cryptophagidae	silken fungus beetles
	Endomychidae	handsome fungus beetles
	Erotylidae	pleasing fungus beetles
	Geotrupidae	earth-boring dung beetles
	Glaphyridae	bumblebee scarab beetles
	Haliplidae	crawling water beetles
	Heteroceridae	variegated mud-loving beetles
	Histeridae	clown beetles
	Hybosoridae	scavenger scarab beetles
	Languriidae	lizard beetles
	Limnichidae	minute marsh-loving beetles
	Lycidae	net-winged beetles
	Lymexylidae	ship-timber beetles
	Nosodendridae	wounded-tree beetles
	Noteridae	burrowing water beetles
	Phalacridae	shining flower beetles
	Psephenidae	water-penny beetles
	Rhysodidae	wrinkled bark beetles
	Scydmaenidae	antlike stone beetles

Further Research

Books

Conniff, Richard. *Spineless Wonders: Strange Tales from the Invertebrate World*. New York: Henry Holt and Company, 1996.

Kneidel, Sally. *Stinkbugs, Stick Insects, and Stag Beetles: And 18 More of the Strangest Insects on Earth*. New York: John Wiley and Sons, 2000.

Nuridsany, Claude and Marie Pérennou. *Microcosmos: The Invisible World of Insects*. New York: Stewart, Tabori & Chang, 1997.

White, Richard E. *A Field Guide to the Beetles of North America* (Peterson Field Guides). Boston: Houghton Mifflin, 1998.

Web Sites

http://www.living-jewels.com/photo.htm
> Many beautiful close-up photos by Poul Beckmann, author of *Living Jewels: The Natural Design of Beetles*.

http://www.ent.iastate.edu/misc/insectsasfood.html
> Insects are high-protein, low-fat foods that people in many cultures eat regularly. To help Americans catch up, Iowa State University has put together some, reportedly, "tasty insect recipes." Parents will appreciate being asked to help.

http://www.ent.iastate.edu/imagegal/coleoptera/
> Iowa State also has a good photo gallery of some crop-relevant beetles. For more beetle information, follow the site to its very good beetles "links" page: http://www.ent.iastate.edu/list/directory/86/vid/5

http://www.nhm.ac.uk/kids-only/naturecams/beetlecam/
index.html
> The flesh-eating beetlecam lets you watch dermestid beetles clean bones for study at the British Natural History Museum.

http://www.fossilmuseum.net/Fossil_Galleries/Insect_Galleries_
by_Order/Coleoptera/coleoptera_fossil_gallery.htm
> It's worth typing the very long Web site address to view this virtual gallery of beetles that have been preserved in amber for tens of millions of years.

http://beetles.source.at/english/navigation.htm
> Two Austrian beetle enthusiasts and photographers display their photos along with an online beetle game and virtual beetle animations.

Bibliography

The author found these books especially helpful when researching this volume.

Agosta, William C. *Bombardier Beetles and Fever Trees*. Reading, MA: Addison-Wesley, 1996.

Berenbaum, May R. *Ninety-nine Gnats, Nits, and Nibblers*. Urbana: University of Illinois Press, 1989.

Evans, Arthur V., and Charles L. Bellamy. *An Inordinate Fondness for Beetles*. Berkeley: University of California Press, 2000.

Milne, Lorus J., and Margery Milne. *Insect Worlds*. New York: Charles Scribner's Sons, 1980.

Waldbauer, Gilbert. *Millions of Monarchs, Bunches of Beetles*. Cambridge, MA: Harvard University Press, 2000.

Index

Page numbers in **boldface** are illustrations.

About the Author

Marc Zabludoff, former editor in chief of *Discover* magazine, has been involved in communicating science to the public for more than two decades. His other work for Marshall Cavendish includes *Spiders* in the AnimalWays series and books on insects, reptiles, and the chiefly microscopic organisms known as protoctists in the Family Trees series. Zabludoff lives in New York City with his wife and daughter, neither of whom has shown any interest in making beetles a steady part of the family diet.